Global
Human Rights

Global Human Rights

People, Processes, and Principles

Peter W. Van Arsdale

University of Denver

WAVELAND

PRESS, INC.

Long Grove, Illinois

For information about this book, contact:
Waveland Press, Inc.
4180 IL Route 83, Suite 101
Long Grove, IL 60047-9580
(847) 634-0081
info@waveland.com
www.waveland.com

Cover: Hani Amir/Shutterstock.com
Unless otherwise noted, all images by the author

Global
Human Rights

Dedicated to Amy Niebling (1975–2005), an American passionary and former student of mine, who died doing what she did best— helping other people at risk. Her accomplishments are highlighted in the concluding chapter.

Dedicated to Haing Ngor (1940–1996),
a Cambodian passionary who left a
powerful legacy for Cambodians and Americans
alike. His story is covered in the first chapter.

Contents

Preface   xiii
Acknowledgements   xv

**Introduction: Night Doctors and   1
Night Commuters**
What Are "Global Human Rights"?   3
People, Processes, and Principles   5
Passionaries, Case Studies, and Activism   5

**1   A Metaphor for Understanding: 7
The "Tree of Rights"**
Essential Principles   7
Structural Violence   10
The Cambodian Doctor   12
   Ngor's Background   12
   The Khmer Rouge: "Revolutionary
     Liberation from Oppression"   13
   Forced Labor   13
   Emergent Genocide   14
   A Tragic Loss   15
   Survival and Escape   16
   Life in the United States   17
Other Important Issues   18

**2   Provision Rights: Water, Sanitation,   21
       and Food Security**

The Necessities of Life   21

Case #1: Kibera and Global WASHES   23

Case #2: Food Insecurity in Somalia   27

Case #3: Water Scarcity at Canyon de Chelly   32

What's Being Done   34
    The World Food Programme in South Sudan   35
    Securing Somalia's Fisheries   36

3   Fragile Bonds: Societal Violence and Warfare   39

Violence Is Personal   39

Case #1: Ethiopia's Red Terror   41

Case #2: Refugees in New Guinea   45

Case #3: India's "Unknown Insurgency"   48

What's Being Done   51
    A Sensible Theory   51
    The Alemu Worku Case   53
    "Cure Violence"   54

**4   Crimes against Humanity: Genocide,   59
       Ethnocide, and Ethnic Cleansing**

Behind Nazi Lines   59

Case #1: Cambodia's Killing Fields   62

Case #2: Genocide in Darfur   65

Case #3: Bosnia's Omarska Concentration Camp   69

What's Being Done   74
    Reengaging Cambodia   74
    Reengaging Darfur   75

5   Invisible Barriers: Children's Rights   77

An Image of God   77

Case #1: Child Abuse, Neglect, and
    Sex Trafficking in the United States   79

Case #2: The Chibok Girls and Boko Haram   82

Case #3: Europe's Missing Refugee Children   85

What's Being Done   89
    A Passionary   89
    An "Honor Killing" that Failed   89
    Tackling Child Abuse and Neglect:
        Models that Work   90

**6   Obligated Actions: Moral and   95
      Material Possibilities**
      An Obligation to Act   95
      Violence: The Worldwide Situation   96
      Champions and Passionaries   97
        Compassion and Risk Taking   98
        Institutional Innovations and Political Diplomacy   99
      The Next Frontier: Gay Rights   101
        Anti-Gay Legislation and Persecution in Africa   101
        The Deaths of African Activists   103
      What's Being Done   104
      Just Do It!   106

      Glossary of Acronyms   109
      Index   111

Preface

This book is intended for both undergraduate and graduate students who are concerned about global human rights. It also is intended for professionals, particularly practitioners who—like me—believe it is imperative to spend lots of time in the field. Some are educators, some are service providers, some are researchers, some are rights advocates, some are humanitarians. This work builds on my involvement in applied anthropology over a 40-year period.

I developed my "Tree of Rights," which is featured in this book, for three reasons: (1) from my frustration with the work of some rights analysts, who seemingly get bogged down in jargon surrounding human rights and their documentation; (2) from my desire to simplify what I see as the essence of global human rights and their evolution, relying heavily on case studies; (3) from my preference to use, whenever possible, visualizations—here, in the form of a diagrammatic tree—to portray key concepts. As I mention in chapter 1, the tree is meant to "guide thought, provoke analysis, and indicate realities."

The roles played by everyday champions and passionaries, who take seriously their obligated actions regarding rights, also are featured. Determined encounters, often under the most difficult of circumstances, are required. I hope readers will ask themselves: What can I do, where can I be most effective, when will the opportunity be right?

Peter W. Van Arsdale
Centennial, Colorado

Acknowledgements

It is important to acknowledge that many nations and international organizations have dedicated a day each year to a human rights, peace, remembrance, independence, or related human welfare issue. Among them, month by month:

January

- Women's Day (Greece)
- Peace Day (El Salvador)
- Martin Luther King's Birthday (United States)

February

- Torture Abolition Day (United Nations)
- Democracy Day (Nepal)
- People Power Day (Philippines)

March

- Liberation Day (Bulgaria)
- Restoration Day (Lithuania)
- Emancipation Day (Puerto Rico)

April

- Ching Ming (China)
- Liberation Day (Uganda)
- Martyrs' Day (Armenia)

May
- Independence Day (Timor-Leste)
- Mother's Day (Canada)
- Cinco de Mayo (Mexico)

June
- Emancipation Day (French Guiana)
- Independence Day (Iceland)
- Martyrs' Day (Togo)

July
- Liberation Day (Rwanda)
- Nelson Mandela's Birthday (South Africa)
- Independence Day (Kiribati)

August
- Revolt of Market Women (Guinea)
- Merdeka Day (Malaysia)
- Independence Day (Moldova)

September
- Children's Day (Honduras)
- Freedom Day (Malta)
- World Peace Day (Baha'i)

October
- Mahatma Gandhi's Birthday (India)
- Liberation Day (Libya)
- Antifascist Day (Macedonia)

November
- Remembrance Day (Bermuda)
- National Peace Day (Côte d'Ivoire)
- Rebirth Day (Estonia)

December
- Human Rights Day (United Nations)
- Independence Day (Portugal)
- Constitution Day (Uzbekistan)

I am appreciative of the valuable assistance I received from four professionals, one of whom also is my daughter. They kindly reviewed and commented on various drafts as the chapters were unfolding:

Edward Antonio, PhD, Andy Dunning, PhD, Edith King, PhD, and Amy Van Arsdale, PhD. Not all of their suggestions have been included, but all have been carefully considered. I also am appreciative of the two editors at Waveland Press whom I've worked with closely: Tom Curtin for the long-standing support he has offered me as an author and applied anthropologist, and Jeni Ogilvie for her thoughtful editorial suggestions and expert copy editing. I am grateful to the many colleagues whom I had the opportunity to interview, and whose ideas and accomplishments are featured herein.

Introduction
Night Doctors and
Night Commuters

"Night, the mother of fear and mystery, was coming."
—H. G. Wells, 1898

"Night doctors" stalk the poor and the oppressed. They kidnap them after dark. Once in captivity, they take them to secret laboratories hidden deep in the bowels of aging medical facilities, there to conduct experiments outside the prying eyes of medical authorities. Night doctors abuse their human rights. Since the 19th century, as Rebecca Skloot (2010) points out, African American oral history has been rife with such ominous stories. While no such night doctors actually existed, and no such abductions actually took place, such fears are rooted in tales told to slaves by plantation owners to keep them from escaping. That some bodies actually were exhumed and used for research complicated the understandings. Some black residents living near the Johns Hopkins School of Medicine in Baltimore, Maryland, believed that the facility—initially funded in 1873—had been built there for the benefit of such night doctors. In fact, the facility had been built there to benefit the residents of poor neighborhoods.

That the legend of night doctors played out so provocatively in Baltimore is ironic. A young man named Freddie Gray was arrested by Baltimore police on April 12, 2015, and suffered a mysterious spine injury while in police custody. He had been handcuffed, shackled by the feet, and left unrestrained by a seat belt to bounce around inside a moving police van. He later died of the injuries he sustained inside the van. A prosecutor brought charges against the six officers involved,

1

and a grand jury indicted them on counts ranging from second-degree murder to involuntary manslaughter. The prosecutor later said there had been no reason to arrest Gray in the first place. The grand jury added charges that the officers had repeatedly failed to assist Gray while he asked for aid (Calamur 2015). As riots broke out in Baltimore, stores were looted and gun-toting citizens guarded their property. A neighbor of one of my anthropology colleagues sat on his front step with a loaded shotgun. In September 2015, the city of Baltimore reached a $6.4 million wrongful death settlement with Gray's family (Alexander 2015). Citizens came to see this not only as a civil rights issue but as a human rights issue.

A very different kind of night doctor actually stalks the hallways of some of Burundi's 35 hospitals. This small East African nation has struggled with economic, political, and ethnic issues, and to some it appears to be a "backwater" to its more progressive neighbor, Rwanda. With a GDP per capita of less than US$300, it is one of the world's poorest countries. The under-five mortality rate is among the world's highest. Its former Belgian overlords did little to bolster its 21st-century prospects, and—while its hospitals do utilize certain modern technologies—their treatment of impoverished patients can be inhumane. As Sarah May (2015) stresses, the government health system provides little stable financial support, and hospitals therefore are largely responsible for self-funding. No systematic programs exist for this. Insolvent patients, along with their children, are sometimes detained within the facilities by doctors as a form of punishment.

Detained patients often are deprived of food and water. They must rely on family or friends to provide these "provision rights" to them. One detainee was quoted as saying, "For me it is difficult to get food. . . . I am waiting for God's help" (quoted in May 2015: 1). As May notes, the detention of indebted patients not only violates universal human rights charters and conventions, it violates the human rights ensconced in the African Charter for Human and People's Rights. Ratified by Burundi in 2004, the charter explicitly prohibits the unlawful or inhumane detention of children. May forcefully argues that depriving children of food, water, or medical treatment while detained in a hospital qualifies as "inhuman" and "degrading." The doctors, some no doubt unwillingly, are serving as accomplices. This is a form of structural violence, a theory detailed in chapter 1.

"Night commuters" were children living in northern Uganda. At the height of Lord's Resistance Army (LRA) raids and child abductions in the 1990s and 2000s, thousands "commuted" nightly from displaced person camps and rural villages to safe havens in larger cities such as Gulu. If abducted by the LRA, they might well—like thousands of others—have become child soldiers, laborers, or sex slaves. As young as three years old and regularly walking as far as 20 kilometers, these children found safety in numbers, in hideouts. They might bed down in an abandoned warehouse, a church, a hospital, or an underground tunnel. They might seek food from sympathetic residents, NGOs, or street vendors; they also might steal it. They often had a nominal leader, an older boy or girl. The international "Invisible Children" campaign, at times controversial in its own right, did much to bring attention to these children's plight. My discussion with some of the campaign's US leaders took place in 2011.

The LRA fought a long-standing battle against the Ugandan government and forcibly sought adult as well as child recruits. Its predecessor movement, the Holy Spirit Mobile Forces, was founded in 1986 by a mystic visionary named Alice Auma-*cum*-Lakwena, whose messianic message and antigovernment battle was later corrupted and intensified by her cousin, Joseph Kony. The army he founded became ruthless in its abuses as it sought revolutionary change. Although displaced from Uganda in 2006, its vestiges remain elsewhere in Central and East Africa. A rare interview (including visuals) with the elusive and abusive Kony was conducted that same year by British journalist Sam Farmar (cited in Wolf 2010). When questioned about documented atrocities ranging from rape to torture to mutilation, Kony replied that these allegations were trumped up by the Ugandan president, Yoweri Museveni, whom Lakwena also had opposed. Kony claimed to be a freedom fighter seeking a free and democratic Uganda (Wolf 2010).

Even night patrols, as conducted by both Allied and Axis military in World War II in the European theater, can result in abuse. A surveillance mission can turn into a point-blank confrontation and the killing of an enemy soldier without remorse. The night obscures certain details, yet magnifies the horror. The destruction of war often correlates with a death machine that takes on a life of its own (Megellas 2003).

Therefore, in this way, nights can introduce us to rights. As Elie Wiesel wrote about the Holocaust, in prefacing his renown book *Night* (1986; orig. 1960), "Everything came to an end—man, history, literature, religion, God. There was nothing left. And yet we begin again with night."

WHAT ARE "GLOBAL HUMAN RIGHTS"?

Global human rights encompass a broad range of rights, of importance to all people. However, they are not "global" in the sense that they always emerge from discussions involving representatives of all (or most) major ethnic groups, or that they are accepted by representatives of all (or most) nation-states. They are global in that they have emerged from the drama, discourse, and debate of many people over many centuries. They span "rights generations," that is, from personal/political to social/group, from those with economic impacts to those with ecological impacts, from those dealing with solidarity to those dealing with intellectual property. Human rights permeate our everyday lives; they are not "unusual," "remote," or "detached."

Human rights did not emerge, preformed, from the primeval ooze. They did not descend from on high, from God or from the gods. They were not "waiting out there, to be discovered" by diligent activists or academics. Human rights evolved over time, as often imperfect attempts to grapple with the human condition and to better enable human survival. Members of diverse societies wrestled with what is good and evil, what is right and wrong, what to do when conditions are peaceful and when they are not. They still do. While there are certain cross-cultural commonalities, there also are certain culture-specific differences.

On a spectrum that analysts see spanning "the absolute universal" to the "absolute relativistic" in terms of rights' applicability, I firmly believe in what is termed "weak cultural relativism." This is a relativism that is culturally contextual and, in part, culturally dependent. "Weak" means that culture is an important source of a particular right's validity, with universality being initially presumed. Not all rights play out in the same way or are interpreted in the same way by members of different societies, but certain universals are sought. Examples are freedom from torture, from slavery, from rendition. From this perspective, rights are mediated by culture-specific values and norms, and rights in turn reflect such values and norms. As an example, freedom of speech for an Asmat woman in Indonesia is not the same as freedom of speech for a Latina woman in the United States. As another example, freedom of movement for a Swiss shepherd is not the same as freedom of movement for a Kababish herdsman.

Analysts wrestle with what is, and what isn't, a human right. They wrestle with questions of justification of torture under special circumstances, of intervention under duress, of assistance to those who themselves might be perpetrators of violence. More generally, professionals wrestle with what constitute "relatives" and "absolutes" (e.g., Twiss 2007). These are important questions but are not addressed in detail here. In a large-circulation Sunday newspaper like that of my hometown of Denver, Colorado *(The Denver Post),* four to five articles related to human rights—whether headlined explicitly with this phrase or not—appear every week: prison riots and prisoner rights, chemical warfare and humanitarian intervention, disabled soldiers and federal legislation to assist them. While these particular issues are not addressed here, they all share commonalities with those I am covering. They deal with at-risk individuals, with purposeful marginalization, with the uses and abuses of power. They occur cross-nationally, cross-culturally, cross-ethnically; they rarely respect political boundaries. They intersect the concerns of activists in the civil rights, social justice, humanitarian, and human rights fields.

PEOPLE, PROCESSES, AND PRINCIPLES

The consideration of human rights goes far beyond the explication of documents, covenants, and protocols (such as the United Nations Universal Declaration of Human Rights). Human rights are about people's struggles and achievements, about their companions and their persecutors. People, processes, and principles are paramount.

I previously served on the Committee for Human Rights of the American Anthropological Association (AAA). At a public forum held several years later, in 2014, members of this committee discussed a Third Declaration on Anthropology and Human Rights. Whereas the first two had been a bit more historical, the third would stress "a more grounded and living document [connecting] research and practice in foundational themes such as inquiry evidence and advocacy . . . [while moving] beyond statism, challenging power and informing public debate" (Friedlander and Unterberger 2015: 20). This effort hopefully will lead to a new version of the AAA Declaration on Human Rights and a crisper delineation of essential principles; I had the privilege of contributing to the earlier version, a process that complemented my thinking on the "Tree of Rights," which is detailed in chapter 1.

PASSIONARIES, CASE STUDIES, AND ACTIVISM

Although recent transnational protocols, covenants, and legal guidelines are extremely important to the understanding of human rights, this text does not emphasize such documents. It is not a book about what guidelines say should be done; it is a book about what people actually have done (and are doing), pro and con. It is about victims like Freddie Gray and perpetrators like Joseph Kony. It is about activists like Helen Abyei and Roz Duman. The central chapters—2, 3, 4, and 5—each feature three primary case studies. Short sidebars feature individual and organizational human rights champions. One term for the individual champions is "passionaries." Coined by Barbara Metzler (2006), this term refers to exceptional people, compassionate visionaries whose positive actions lead to significant changes in the lives of others. Occasionally these passionaries become well-known, but more often they do not. They do not seek the limelight. At times their efforts are confounded by political, economic, and/or cultural constraints. Risk often is involved in their work. Determined encounters and persistence are hallmarks of their actions. Improved human rights and improved human welfare are their primary concerns. In keeping with a real-world, activist theme, a number of the featured individuals are people I know. Several of the organizations are ones I have worked with or personally encountered in the field. Their "best practices," their knowledge of "what works," is stressed.

Alexander, Keith L. 2015. Baltimore reaches $6.4 million settlement with Freddie Gray family. *The Washington Post,* September 8. Retrieved from https://www.washingtonpost.com/local/crime/baltimore-reaches-64-million-settlement-with-freddie-grays-family/2015/09/08/80b2c092-5196-11e5-8c19-0b6825aa4a3a_story.html

Calamur, Krishnadev. 2015. Grand jury indicts 6 Baltimore officers in Freddie Gray's death. *Breaking news from NPR News* (May 21). Retrieved from http://www.npr.org/sections/thetwo-way/2015/05/21/408567971/grand-jury-indicts-6-baltimore-officers-in-freddie-grays-death

Friedlander, Eva and Alayne Unterberger. 2015. News you can use: What's ahead for 2015 in human rights. *Anthropology News* 56(3/4): 20.

May, Sarah. 2015. *"Since you have not paid, we will imprison you": Detention in Burundian hospitals.* Unpublished manuscript, Josef Korbel School of International Studies, University of Denver, Denver, CO.

Megellas, James. 2003. *All the way to Berlin: A paratrooper at war in Europe.* New York: Ballantine Books.

Metzler, Barbara R. 2006. *Passionaries: Turning compassion into action.* West Conshohocken, PA: Templeton Foundation Press.

Skloot, Rebecca. 2010. *The immortal life of Henrietta Lacks.* New York: Crown.

Twiss, Sumner B. 2007. Torture, justification, and human rights: Toward an absolute proscription. *Human Rights Quarterly* 29(2): 346–367. (Abstracted online at Collaborative Refugee and Rights Information Center [CRRIC], University of Denver, by Annmarie Barnes.)

Wells, H. G. 2015 [orig. 1898]. *The war of the worlds.* New York: Atria Unbound.

Wiesel, Elie. 1986 [orig. 1960]. *Night* (translated by Stella Rodway). New York: Bantam Books.

Wolf, Kristen. 2010. Joseph Kony: First ever interview by journalist [Sam Farmar]. *American Anthropologist* 112(2): 137.

Chapter One

A Metaphor for Understanding
The "Tree of Rights"

ESSENTIAL PRINCIPLES

My "Tree of Rights" serves as a metaphor (see the diagram on the following page). It offers a communitarian vision, illustrating the evolutionary nature of human rights in diverse cultural settings, as we wrestle with how best to help one another. The tree demonstrates that rights are continually growing and changing. Just as a tree is never static, neither are rights. The tree is meant to be universal, while not suggesting that all specific rights unfold in the same manner. This metaphor can be used in several ways, but particularly as an educational tool. The tree provides a baseline, a touchstone, for this book.

The roots of the Tree of Rights represent needs or *provision rights*—these rights are strikingly different from rights represented higher in the tree, like the right to be free from slavery. Provision rights are foundational necessities for basic human functioning: water, sanitation, food, shelter. The first three of these are covered in chapter 2. Deep in the trunk of the tree are *debate* and *discourse,* which build on culture-specific human experiences. These processes are essential; the remainder of what is represented in the tree's limbs and branches depends on them. From these come new rights, changes in the perception of rights, and the reframing of rights cross-culturally. Rights ide-

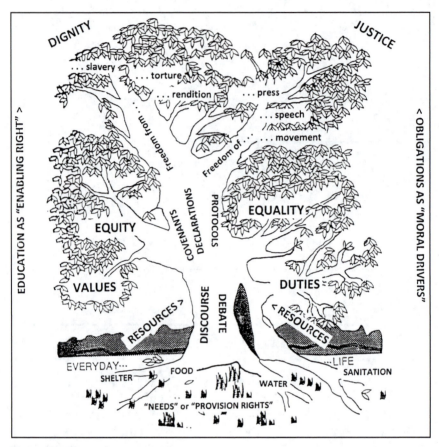

Tree of Rights.

ally must be evidentiary: based on truth, fact, or reality that is empirically derived—observed or experienced.

Rights cannot be tackled without resources. These support the trunk of the tree. Resources are of three kinds: (1) *human*, represented by the skilled advocates who move a cause forward; (2) *networks*, represented by the interactive, often transnational organizations, associations, and alliances that partner to address the toughest issues and ultimately improve rights-based laws; and (3) *funds*, reflected in state-funded mandates that enact policies, in programs run by IGOs (intergovernmental organizations), and in voluntary contributions that come from committed individuals, philanthropies, and NGOs (nongovernmental organizations).

Rights continually evolve and emerge through discourse, debate, and analysis. These discourses occur within legal frameworks (e.g., in court cases and tribunals) but also outside of such frameworks—in classrooms, service agencies, and general society. These debates often lead to *covenants, protocols,* and *declarations* of importance. The covenants and related conventions usually encompass specific rights represented in the branches of the tree. For example, the International Convention on the Elimination of All Forms of Racial Discrimination includes elements such as the right to equal treatment before tribunals and all other organs administering justice, and the right to freedom of speech, conscience, and religion. Framing the tree is *education,* as this enables other rights to be analyzed, interpreted, and debated. Education is the most important enabling right. Also framing the tree is *obligation,* referring to the mandate for those with resources to assist those without, who are under duress. This is detailed in the book's final chapter.

Equality and *equity* are essential principles ensconced in the tree. As I conceive it, equality means that every person—no matter status, role, or ability—is entitled to the same basic human rights. (It does not mean that every person is equivalent, in a broader sense, to every other person. Human diversity prevails.) Equity relates to fairness and, in actual practice as I conceive it, is the more important of the two principles. Fairness recognizes the differentials that exist among people. As related to resource access, in the context of torture, for example, it mandates that each at-risk person be individually evaluated and individually assisted. It requires the careful evaluation of an at-risk person's circumstances, recognizing that, for example, a woman in Pakistan who has been raped will require assistance that differs from that afforded a woman in Mozambique who has been raped.

Appropriately "above the tree tops" are *dignity* and *justice.* These epitomize what the Tree of Rights, and thus rights themselves, are all about. The former plays out more in a personal context, the latter more in an institutional context. I believe that these are the two most important outcomes of rights-based research, education, training, advocacy, intervention, and policy making. Dignity reflects self-awareness and self-respect. Its sister concept is autonomy, referring to the valued independence of the person in mind, body, and spirit. In tandem, dignity and autonomy indicate a personal sanctity that is not to be violated by others. The two concepts are inextricably linked and represent "what ideally should be." Justice emphasizes doing what is right for people at risk, "righting a wrong" institutionally, to enable their full-fledged and enriched survival. It encompasses benevolence—compassionate assistance to those in severe need—and nonmalevolence—assistance that does not lead to secondary negative consequences (such as the violation of privacy). When actualized, justice restrains those in power from exacting evil on the powerless. "It calls for acts which demonstrate compassion and ameliorate suffering. It mandates aggressive efforts to overturn structural inequalities and

structural violence [see below]. It mandates a determined encounter"
(Van Arsdale 2006: 184–185).

In the introduction, the notion of "weak cultural relativism" was
explained. The Tree of Rights supports and accommodates this. As the
various limbs and branches on the tree suggest, rights emerge and
vary, through time and across cultures. As mentioned, not all rights
play out in the same way, but key universals are sought. To paraphrase Amartya Sen, these universals have to do with human beings'
fundamental rights to develop and maximize their capabilities, processes that link them to the development of societies and nations (Sen
1999). All rights are *value-mediated*. Ethical persons who work dili-
gently to implement them are *duty bound*. Both negative and positive
rights are represented on the tree. "Negative" are those such as slavery, which states, institutions, and individuals work to prevent; a person should not be subjected to these. "Positive" are those such as free
speech, which states, institutions, and individuals work to promote; a
person should be afforded these.

Not all rights are represented on this ever-changing tree. As a
metaphor, the tree is meant to guide thought, provoke analysis, and
indicate realities, not be all-encompassing. A very important right not
represented is that involving property. Some would argue that a property right in oneself serves as a guarantor of other rights because it
defines a "sphere of autonomy" around a person (Ghosh 2012). Others
would argue that property, as reflected in one's land and possessions,
lends stability and provides support, such that other essential tasks
can be accomplished. This also encompasses a notion of autonomy.
Another important right not included on the tree, which complements
the "sphere of autonomy" concept, involves privacy. To be able to sit on
a log, out in the sun, and not be disturbed, is meaningful. To be able to
go into one's home, and not be invaded, is essential.

STRUCTURAL VIOLENCE

If there is a single theory that best circumscribes the human
rights interests of applied anthropologists, that best transcends community, institutional, governmental, and academic concerns, and that
best yields understandings across the board, it is that of *structural
violence*. It complements the metaphorical tree. Following the innovative writings of Paul Farmer (2003), who grounded himself in the sem-
inal work of Johan Galtung and Amartya Sen, I have laid out five
central premises of structural violence (Van Arsdale 2006: 6): (1) Differential power relations within society create structural inequalities;
(2) these inequalities become institutionalized by elites and create

This baobab tree—locally known as *tebelde*—serves as a sentinel in Sudan's western savanna. It also inspired me, as I first conceptualized my "Tree of Rights."

oppressive conditions that, in turn, lead to human rights violations; (3) structural inequalities and structural violence are linked; (4) structural violence is not always exhibited through harshly aggressive physical processes (i.e., "guns, maiming, and killing") but in the everyday circumstances that confront people who are at risk in oppressive environments; (5) disproportionate access to needed resources is linked to disproportionate risk, the kind of risk that is seen in suffering and death among those least able to advocate for systemic change. Structural violence is not always physically violent, but it engages and legitimizes institutions that oppress and that systematically disadvantage at-risk people. It compromises human rights, and it commodifies people. Bodies, labor, and lives become "useful objects of exchange and exploitation" (Vogt 2013: 765).

The theory of structural violence, considered in conjunction with the principles of dignity and justice, therefore provides insights into what constitutes a rights violation. If the institutional elite oppress a person, dignity is restricted; this is a rights violation. If a coercive system of labor is developed, autonomy is constrained; this is a rights violation. If someone is subjected to false imprisonment, and appropriate legal representation is absent, justice is suborned; this is a rights violation. If a person is trafficked and sold, he or she is commodifed; this is a rights violation. Each of these represents structural inequalities and abuses. Again referencing Sen, if one is not allowed to maximize his or her capabilities, which include the fresh experience of life without oppression, this is a rights violation. These are the universal issues that "weak cultural relativism" addresses.

> *"Human rights matter because they . . . reveal violence in its structural and overt forms."*
> —Jaymelee Kim, 2016 (quoted in Unterberger)

THE CAMBODIAN DOCTOR

Hannah Arendt, one of the world's great rights advocates, stressed that all people have "a right to have rights," yet rightlessness—as for forcibly displaced migrants—seemingly persists (Gündogdu 2015). This is what Haing Ngor encountered and what he ultimately overcame, as he battled the structural—and at times spectacular—violence engendered by the Cambodian genocide in 1975–1979.

This book is codedicated to the memory Haing Ngor, a true "passionary" as defined in the introduction. I met him in 1992. A physician in his native Cambodia, he was forced to flee Phnom Penh, to leave his medical practice behind, and to take on the pseudorole of taxi driver. The genocidal activities of the Khmer Rouge in the late 1970s forced him to transmogrify himself completely. His life was changed, but he scrapped, he scraped, and he survived. He was tortured, imprisoned, and forced to watch the torture and murder of others. There were many times, as he reported in his gripping 1987 book, *Haing Ngor: A Cambodian Odyssey*, when he wished he had not lived. While details of the Cambodian genocide are presented in chapter 4 herein, in honor of Ngor I present portions of his personal story here. Some are drawn from my interview of him; most are taken from his memoir. The pursuit of dignity and justice, keys to the Tree of Rights, were essential to his survival.

Ngor's Background

Ngor had led a relatively privileged life. Born in 1940, he grew up in the village of Samrong Nong, outside the Cambodian capital, Phnom Penh. Early on, he also spent "safe time" in the capital, because even then—long before the genocide—there were political tensions. Some of these were tied to "color politics" and interethnic problems; others were due to pressures exerted by French colonialists. His father was kidnapped more than once. That Ngor excelled at both school and gang fighting would stand him well later on. That he was clever at "earning an extra buck" also would stand him well. That he was tortured by police seeking extortion money toughened him up, and gave him a glimpse of things to come.

Ngor entered medical school in the late 1960s and, while there, also began tutoring. One of his most promising students was a young woman named Chang My Huoy. Mutually intrigued but cautious, a year later a romance began, and a year after that, they were married. Brewing political tensions, of a kind different than had been seen under the French, embroiled them from that day forward. Political convulsions, retributions, and realignments—coming from at least three directions, as noted in chapter 4—in one sense brought "traditional Cambodia" to a halt and in another sense "revolutionary Cambodia" to a start.

The Khmer Rouge: "Revolutionary Liberation from Oppression"

"April 17, 1975, is a day of great victory of tremendous historical significance for our Cambodian nation and people!" shouted a leader of the revolutionary Khmer Rouge, who were sweeping into power. "Long live the line of absolute struggle, independence, self-reliance and overcoming all obstacles," shouted a woman in reply (Ngor 1987: 91). Another speaker whom Ngor heard stated that Cambodia was under a new regime, called Democratic Kampuchea, and that there would be no rich and no poor. Everyone would be equal. All must sacrifice for Angka, a nondescript and amorphous entity of presumably great power. To accomplish this, urban residents must become rural dwellers. Cities must be abandoned. Professionals must become farmers. New laws must be implemented. New soldiers would assure compliance. Those who did not follow orders would be punished. The "revolutionary liberation from oppression" had begun. In fact, the structural violence had begun. The "liberation" would last for four genocidal years. This campaign would be led by a former carpenter turned political organizer named Saloth Sar, whose brutality soon would be compared to that of Stalin and Hitler. He had taken the pseudonym Pol Pot.

Surprisingly, there was little active resistance to the "liberation." A Buddhist passivism and acceptance set in. As thousands formed a day/night exodus from Phnom Penh (among many cities), heading in various directions, Ngor quickly went from being a respected doctor driving a Mercedes to being a straggler wearing rubber sandals and carrying a rucksack. Since food was not provided initially, stealing quickly became necessary. Warehouses soon were stripped bare of provisions like rice. Order became disorder, compliance became chaos, collaborators became competitors. Most highways and roads were jammed with people trudging to as-yet-unknown rural destinations. They were becoming rightless.

Forced Labor

Once ensconced in the countryside, Ngor and his wife Huoy were forced to dig irrigation canals. He disguised his former identity as a

doctor, claiming to be a taxi driver, having heard that such well-edu-
cated professionals were being tortured, even killed. Each "new
farmer" used a simple hoe. The goal in this area was to capture and
divert enough water to grow three—not merely the standard two—rice
crops annually. (I know how difficult it is to achieve three, having
studied the process elsewhere in Southeast Asia [Van Arsdale and
Lewis 1995]). Their day began as early as 4:30 A.M. and ended as late
as 12:00 midnight. They marched to the fields in well-organized ranks,
a kind of communist vision of worker harmony. Cigarette smoking, as
well as marijuana for some, preoccupied their work breaks. An ever-
present loudspeaker blared: "Bright red blood . . . covers towns and
plains of Kampuchea, our motherland. . . . We are uniting to build
splendid Democratic Kampuchea" (Ngor 1987: 206–207).

Food was ladled out in small, carefully measured proportions by
team leaders. The workers—war slaves, as Ngor called his fellow men
and women—fought constantly over what constituted fair amounts. If
necessary, they traded tobacco for food. Almost daily, Khmer Rouge
soldiers would drag two or three workers away. Had they stolen food?
Had they spoken against Angka? Most disappeared, never to be seen
again. In nightly meetings, the workers were exhorted to work harder,
to beware of American CIA agents. Yet there were no such agents, only
Khmer Rouge *chhlop* (spies). Some were as young as 12.

Emergent Genocide

Ngor had hidden a bit of extra food. Two *chhlop* caught him. He
was accused of antirevolutionary behavior by not sharing. Led to a
jungle prison and tied to a mango tree, he was left to the red ants,
which bit him severely. Other war slaves were tied up nearby. A burly
interrogator demanded to know why he had stolen food, and why he
was obviously lying about having been a taxi driver. The tip of his fin-
ger was then chopped off "for stealing." His ankle was then beaten and
damaged "for being greedy." Women were treated just as harshly, some
much more so. One pregnant woman was disemboweled, her fetus
hung from the prison eaves. Another woman, who survived, had her
fingernails ripped out.

These are the acts that accompany genocide. This is how fear is
instilled in the innocent. Nearly two million Cambodians ultimately
died or disappeared. Ngor was released, to return to his wife and the
other workers. His torturers no doubt hoped he would tell the other
workers about what had happened, to keep them in line. The "new
people," most of them farmers, paradoxically were to be both worked
hard and destroyed. As time went on, the act of killing became rou-
tine, part of the job. The leader of Ngor's work cooperative, an older
man named Char, did it discreetly, apparently murdering with his
farming hoe. He was doing his duty to Angka. Younger soldiers seem-

ingly killed just to obey orders, almost automatically. Others were sadists. "Torturing others was the ultimate proof of their own power" (Ngor 1987: 230).

One of the omnipotent Angka's power brokers was informally known as the "King of Death." An informant tipped him off that Ngor had been a doctor. He was taken to a kangaroo court; a confession was demanded. Since none was forthcoming, the King's assistants kicked him, beat him, and took him to a field with 17 others, to be crucified. One-by-one, prisoners were hung on crosses fixed to old soccer goal posts. Using dried rice husks, fires were started beneath their feet. Insects swarmed over their bodies. Some survived a few hours, and others—miraculously like Ngor—a few days and then were removed. Survivors were interrogated again. A noncompliant woman next to him was disemboweled.

A Tragic Loss

At one point along the way, in order to survive, Ngor and Huoy secretly took on the roles of servants. A farmer named Youen agreed to take them in, as long as they would not make trouble and perform their chores well. Having taken the name "Samnang" (which means "lucky"), Ngor felt fortunate to have found a rural backwater where he would not be facing the front lines and where he would not be scrutinized too closely. Youen had no inkling that Ngor actually was a doctor. In an ironic twist, in times past, Youen (the farmer) would have had to bow and be extremely deferential to Ngor (the doctor). Now, "Samnang" bowed deferentially to Youen. To gain a bit of permanency, Ngor and Huoy built a simple hut in Youen's village. They were able to get enough rice to eat moderately well. It was Ngor's understanding that, as servants, they would be protected. But soon the Khmer Rouge began a secondary mobilization, and Ngor and Huoy were forced to the front lines.

Conditions continued to worsen during the first three years of the Khmer Rouge regime. Food became increasingly scarce, yet the war slaves were expected to work even harder. No letters in or out were allowed. Rumors of everything from mass killings to cannibalism circulated. When Huoy became pregnant, she and her husband shared both joy and fear. Then Huoy learned of the death of her mother and began a slow, downward decline. She worried constantly about the *chhlop*. As the time for the birth approached, she began to experience a variety of health problems, exacerbated by malnutrition. A Cesarean was necessary, but ironically, despite Ngor's expertise as a doctor, there was no medical equipment and no way to evade the eyes of the *chhlop* (who likely would have killed him for exposing his long-suspected medical skills). Huoy and her child died during childbirth on June 2, 1978.

Survival and Escape

After Huoy's death, Ngor was torn by grief and remorse. He returned to a work crew. He helped with crop fertilization. But his survival meant further secretive activity. With his "stealing partner," a man named Tha, he succeeded in leading gangs of hungry men to a mountain garden where crops were abundant. They also managed to steal a good deal of rice, which they hid under a pile of fertilizer. When an informant named Pen Tip fingered him, he creatively evaded the inevitable *kum* (revenge). He felt increasingly desperate yet increasingly empowered. As the months went on, Ngor became convinced that he must escape Cambodia entirely, no matter the risk. When he heard, in December 1978, that Khmer Serei ("Free Khmer," an anticommunist resistance group) apparently would be launching attacks to free the people living along the Thai border, he was elated. Still, escaping—rather than waiting—would be the necessary choice for him. In this his dignity could be saved.

Yet, surprisingly, by early 1979 it proved to be the reviled Vietnamese who were the actual liberators. Substantial Khmer Serei support never materialized. In yet another irony, it appeared to Ngor that Vietnamese communists, of one stripe, were intent on driving out Khmer Rouge communists, of a different stripe. Their recent success against American forces certainly had emboldened the Vietnamese, who now were teaming with Cambodian liberators whose precise roles were ill-defined. In yet the next irony, when the liberators encountered Ngor and his colleagues, the "liberators" tied them up and herded them toward the town of Battambang. He wondered: Is this liberation? Is this also because I am part Chinese? As he trudged off, arms bound, he noted the date; it was coincidentally four years to the day since the revolution had begun.

In Battambang, as elsewhere in Cambodia, things were opening up. The Khmer Rouge were in retreat. Their mass slaughters had ended. Their plans for a new agricultural state of equals were in shambles. The regime of Heng Samrin was taking over, in alliance with the Vietnamese. Cities were being repopulated, economic opportunities were appearing, and moments of gaiety could be seen. With word again out that Ngor was, in actuality, a doctor and not a taxi driver, he was approached by Battambang's governor to see if he would accept a posting at its hospital. His old professor once had taught there. After wavering, he reluctantly accepted but stayed only a short time. This new Cambodia, even if free of genocide, had no appeal. It offered no justice. His wife and many family members were dead. He was reformulating his plan of escape.

Ngor actualized his plan shortly thereafter. During the following weeks, he and thousands of other potential refugees headed for the so-called Danger Zone, near the Cambodia–Thailand border. They walked day and night. The jungles and mountains were known to be nearly impassable unless a guide—a *coyote*—was employed. Ngor and his small group interviewed prospective *coyotes* as they neared the Dangrek Mountains, and finally settled on a man whose team would charge them "only" about US$2,000. Having hidden small pieces of gold in their clothing, each person paid his or her share. Yet, as they moved out, it became clear that the guides were less than trustworthy and that the liberating soldiers of the Heng Samrin regime had something other than refugee protection on their minds. By his count, on nearly 40 occasions they were stopped, harassed, robbed, and abused by soldiers, bandits, and border guards. Several times female members of their group were raped. The *coyotes* abandoned them long before they reached the border. Several members of nearby groups that were fleeing were killed when they stepped on land mines. At one point Ngor thought—apart from mass murders—that what they were encountering was worse than what had happened under the Khmer Rouge.

After weeks on foot, Ngor and the surviving members of his group made it to the Nong Chan refugee camp inside the Thai border. Using a bit of gold that he had saved, he treated each of those around him to an ice-cold Pepsi Cola—and then to another. A few weeks after arriving, in June 1979, he and others were transferred to Bangkok, the Thai capital. He began working in one of the medical clinics as a volunteer doctor. That opened other doors for him. He later worked as a paid doctor in the emergent Khao-I-Dang refugee camp. (This camp grew to become the then-largest in the world, housing Cambodian refugees.) Nearly a year after that, with the assistance of an American official, he was given permission to fly to the United States. Using transit number 33144, he boarded his flight on August 30, 1980. Two days later, the refugee Haing Ngor arrived in California.

Life in the United States

Coincidentally, at about this same time, a journalist named Sydney Schanberg published an article in *The New York Times Magazine* about a remarkable Cambodian colleague and genocide survivor named Dith Pran. Pran had saved Schanberg and several other Western journalists from execution at the hands of the Khmer Rouge. He also had experienced many of same horrors as a "new farmer" that Ngor had. One thing led to another, and in 1983 when the English producer David Puttnam decided to make a feature film based on the story, Haing Ngor was chosen to play the role of Dith Pran. He had never studied acting and—apart from those cameras of his friends and professional colleagues—had never stood before a camera. In short, he was a natural, untarnished by Hollywood. The film *The Killing Fields* was released in 1984 and went on to win three Academy Awards. Ngor was the most surprised of the recipients, winning an Oscar for Best

Supporting Actor. As the filming unfolded, director Roland Joffé advised him to "just be yourself. You were there."

Having established himself in the United States as both actor and human rights activist, now a proponent of justice for other Cambodians, Ngor's greatest personal tragedy ironically was yet to come. On February 25, 1996, just four years after we had met, he was confronted on a Los Angeles street by three reputed members of the "Oriental Lazy Boyz" street gang. He willingly handed over his gold Rolex watch, but when they demanded the locket containing a picture of his wife Huoy, he refused. He was killed on the spot. In the final irony, the three murderers, Tak Sun Tan, Jason Chin, and Indra Lim, were convicted on the same day—April 16, 1998—that Pol Pot's death in Cambodia was confirmed. Angka was no more.

"Oppression and misused power cannot have the last word."
—Rev. Stacy Collins, 2015

OTHER IMPORTANT ISSUES

Among the many important, contemporary human rights issues not covered in this book are lethal injections of US death row inmates, the recent use of chemical weapons (specifically chlorine, sarin, and ricin) in Syria, the long-standing abuse of shipyard laborers in Bangladesh, the subjugation of intellectual property rights of indigenous Amazonian peoples, the treatment of Dalit women in India, the Brothers Home abuse of South Korean children, and the abuse of women in Pakistan (so powerfully portrayed in the 2012 Academy Award-winning documentary, *Saving Face,* directed by Daniel Junge and Sharmeen Obaid-Chinoy). The list seems endless.

Entire fields of "rights endeavor" are opening up. Although not detailed herein, one involves the intersection of cultural heritage and archaeology. The last few years have seen the purposeful destruction of archaeological heritage sites, such as those at Palmyra in Syria, by ISIS. "No designation of sanctity, by God or by UNESCO, suffices to protect the past. The past is helpless," stresses Leon Wieseltier (2015: 72). Through representation of heritage, a people's culture and identity are maintained. Their rights are mirrored. Although not targeted for the same purpose, the same result has obtained in Yemen. A coalition of states, led by Saudi Arabia, began bombing Yemen in March 2015. The stated aim was the reinstatement of the former interim president. Yet, traditional houses in the Old City of Sanaa, a UN World Heritage Site, were destroyed (Varisco 2016).

Another field of rights endeavor involves the intersection of environmental justice and women's rights. For example, large-scale energy development and hydropower projects bring male workers to the community, thereby creating gender dynamics that can decrease women's rights to free movement and increase their exposure to sexually transmitted diseases. Vietnamese women are among those tackling this, aided by Global Greengrants (2015). Another field of rights endeavor involves the intersection of modern art and freedom of expression. For example, dissident artist Ai Weiwei has battled the Chinese government regarding the right to display art that reflects liberal views of social activism. He has been arrested and released, vilified from within, and extolled from without. His criticism of the Chinese government's handling of responses to the 2008 Sichuan earthquake, as children suffered, exacerbated his situation (Ng 2011). Yet another field of rights endeavor involves the intersection of gender and negotiated identity. Chapter 6 does address gay rights issues in discussions of laws and abuses in three African countries but does not engage the other, equally important rights associated with the LGBTQ movement. While problems of societal acceptance remain, remarkable progress has been made in the United States and elsewhere. As one example, a transgender woman named Ruby Corado received a $350,000 grant to open a 10-bed home for 18–24-year-old homeless transgender youth in Washington, DC. Acceptance within the home is guaranteed; acceptance within the neighborhood is improving (Sreenivasan 2015). As another example, in my home state of Colorado, a nine-year-old transgender child named Elsa is representing "truegender." Called a boy at birth, she is living—with the full support of her parents—as a girl; it is her choice (Brown 2015).

> *"I am here . . . as a brother, to share your situation and to make it my own."*
> —Pope Francis, to inmates at the Curren-Fromhold Correction Facility in Philadelphia, September 27, 2015 (quoted in Heller)

Brown, Jennifer. 2015. Transgender in Colorado: Elsa's story. *The Denver Post*, July 19, 1A, 12A–13A.

Collins, Stacy. 2015. Oppression, power, and peace. Prayer presented at St. Andrew United Methodist Church, Highlands Ranch, Colorado, November 8.

Farmer, Paul. 2003. *Pathologies of power: Health, human rights, and the new war on the poor.* Berkeley, CA: University of California Press.

Ghosh, Shubha. 2012. *Identity, invention, and the culture of personalized medicine patenting.* New York: Cambridge University Press.

Global Greengrants. 2015. *Climate justice and women's rights: A guide to supporting grassroots women's actions.* Global Greengrants Fund, Boulder, Colorado. Retrieved from http://www.womenandclimate.org/wp-content/uploads/2015/03/Climate-Justice-and-Womens-Rights-Guide1.pdf

Gündogdu, Ayten. 2015. *Rightlessness in an age of rights: Hannah Arendt and the contemporary struggles of migrants.* Oxford: Oxford University Press.

Heller, Karen. 2015. Inside a Philadelphia prison, the pope offers inmates hope and redemption. *The Washington Post,* September 27. Retrieved from https://www.washingtonpost.com/lifestyle/style/inside-the-philadelphia-prison-that-will-host-pope-francis-on-sunday/2015/09/26/25024fae-5bca-11e5-9757-e49273f05f65_story.html?postshare=8781443366046980&tid=a_inl

Ng, David. 2011. Chinese state media say artist Ai Weiwei released from detainment. *Los Angeles Times,* June 22. Retrieved from http://latimesblogs.latimes.com/culturemonster/2011/06/chinese-media-reports-artist-ai-weiwei-released-from-prison.html

Ngor, Haing (with Roger Warner). 1987. *Haing Ngor: A Cambodian odyssey.* New York: Warner Books.

Sen, Amartya. 1999. *Development as freedom.* New York: Alfred A. Knopf.

Sreenivasan, Hari (correspondent). 2015. Giving homeless transgender youth a safe haven from the streets. *PBS Newshour* (May 22). Retrieved from http://www.pbs.org/newshour/bb/giving-homeless-transgender-youth-safe-haven-streets

Unterberger, Alayne. 2016. Human rights matter! *Anthropology News* 57(3/4): 19.

Van Arsdale, Peter W. 2006. *Forced to flee: Human rights and human wrongs in refugee homelands.* Lanham, MD: Lexington Books.

Van Arsdale, Peter and Tony Lewis. 1995. Triple-crop rice farming in Java: Implications for sustainable development. *Journal of Sustainable Agriculture* 6(1): 5–21.

Varisco, Daniel Martin. 2016. The road to Kawkaban. *Anthropology News* (online). March 24.

Vogt, Wendy A. 2013. Crossing Mexico: Structural violence and the commodification of undocumented Central American migrants. *American Ethnologist* 40(4): 764–780.

Wieseltier, Leon. 2015. The rubble of Palmyra. *The Atlantic* 316 (September 2): 72–76.

Chapter Two

Provision Rights
Water, Sanitation,
and Food Security

THE NECESSITIES OF LIFE

Foundational to the Tree of Rights are the four provision rights: water, sanitation, food, and shelter. This metaphor indicates that, without these, other rights cannot be pursued. Put simply, these provisions are needed for human survival. The following comments are both illustrative and stark. Michael Moroto Lomalinga, chief of Kenya's Daasanach people, perceives an intricate link among water, peace, and survival. These factors are precarious on the shores of Lake Turkana, where they live. As both water levels and water purity decrease, and harsh governmental policies increase, he sees greater problems for his people. "We are not officially counted. . . . We are listed as 'other' in the census. . . . We Daasanach are a marginalized people" (Shea 2015: 68).

That access to potable water is recognized as a human right by many NGOs is not surprising. Other nonprofits, government agencies, and academic institutions take the same stance. That PepsiCo was the first major multinational corporation to concur is surprising, given its earlier more insular stance on international development. As Rotary International stresses, water and sanitation must be dealt with concurrently. As one of my Rotary colleagues, Mike Hitchcock, put it: "Water is sexy. It attracts attention. Sanitation is not sexy. It attracts much less attention, but it's absolutely essential." The plight of children can serve as a particularly powerful impetus for change. Diarrhea causes the death of one in five children in the developing world, a direct result of not having adequate access to clean water and sanitation (Loeb and Botta 2011).

In this chapter, the first three provision rights—water, sanitation, food—are addressed in detail. Shelter is only touched on briefly. Regarding the latter, the comments of another of my colleagues, John Nyawara, are poignant. He lives in Kibera, Kenya, an informal settle-

AGENCY ACTION   El Porvenir

The nonprofit El Porvenir has been working in Nicaragua for 25 years. According to Jenna Saldaña, former director of U.S. operations, it "empowers rural Nicaraguan communities to improve their living standards and reduce burdens on women through the sustainable development of clean water, sanitation, and cooking systems; watershed protection; and health education" (Saldaña 2014). Three key principles guide the organization's work: (1) community empowerment through active participation/ownership in all project phases; (2) creation of sustainable community-based organizations to manage resources; (3) utilization of appropriate technology using low-cost resources. Education, an enabling right (as indicated on the Tree of Rights), is central. These complement the worldwide WASH (water, sanitation, hygiene) improvement movement.

Latrine development has been among the most challenging issues. Composting latrines have problems, and so El Porvenir is featuring double-pit (now prefab) latrines, one per household. Installed for about US$450 each (excluding in-kind labor), these have 25+-year anticipated lifetimes. Over 500 were installed in 2014 alone. As Saldaña stressed, sanitation "sells less well than water" (for funders and community activists alike) and so "creative marketing" is essential. The organization's local staff turnover has been of moderate concern, and so certain incentives are used, such as the gift of a shovel for a staffer who helps dig the latrine pit. She stressed that the top three ways to improve health in developing nations such as Nicaragua are hand washing, improved sanitation, and use of clean water. According to WHO, integrated WASH approaches reduce the number of deaths caused by diarrheal diseases by 65%. "Best practices" include (1) implementing projects only when locally requested, based on "felt needs"; (2) using appropriate technologies, with OM&R paramount; (3) involving community water-and-sanitation committees fully; (4) communities paying a portion of project costs; (5) using outside evaluators to assess project effectiveness.

Community participation and coleadership therefore are essential. During 2014 over 20,000 Nicaraguans partnered with El Porvenir on sanitation, water, health education, and watershed management projects. Most served as volunteers.

ment that is dealt with in detail in this chapter. "A house is essential. A home is even better. When my wife and I married, and my income improved, we didn't move out. We moved up [to a slightly better place within Kibera]."

CASE #1: KIBERA AND GLOBAL WASHES

By some estimates, nearly two-thirds of the sub-Saharan African urban population live in informal settlements (sometimes referred to as slums) or suffer from one or more of the five so-called "shelter deprivations" that define a slum. These are access to improved water, access to improved sanitation facilities, sufficient living area, structural quality of buildings, and security of tenure (United Nations 2008). Regarding sanitation, Lacey Stone of UNICEF (2015) indicates that 36 percent of the world's population—about 2.5 billion people—lack improved sanitation facilities. To improve the situation, analyses at the settlement and household levels are paramount.

Among the fastest-growing informal settlements have been those in and around Nairobi, the Kenyan capital. One of the best-known is Kibera. Originally settled by Nubian immigrants from the Sudan/Kenya border region, residents of the settlement now also include members of the Kikuyu, Luo, and other ethnic groups. The vast majority do not own the extraordinarily modest homes they occupy. Kibera is among the most densely populated places on earth, with an estimated 500,000 people living in an area of slightly more than one square mile. Essential services are inadequate, with government-sponsored electrification, water, sewer, trash, and road maintenance being almost nonexistent. Yet, numerous NGOs, service organizations, and schools are operating. Administratively, the settlement is divided into 12 villages, one of the most prominent of which is Silanga. It is headed by a chief whom everyone calls Patrick. It has a population of about 75,000.

When I visited Silanga, I was taken into its heart by a Kenyan colleague. In addition to his enthusiasm for "wat/san" (i.e., water and sanitation issues), he said he needed to accompany me for three reasons: (1) so that I wouldn't get lost. Paths, alleys, and the few roads that can accommodate vehicles twist in seemingly impossible directions, without signs, and it is easy to get confused; (2) so that I wouldn't get attacked. He said that foreign visitors occasionally are unwelcome; (3) so that I'd see "the real Kibera, without varnish." Open sewers were hard to avoid, but as I stepped over one, a drunken woman accosted me. A few minutes later, another woman—an elementary school teacher wearing a bright red dress—engaged me in lively conversation. A few minutes after that, I chatted with a group of young men playing checkers in the heat of the day; each was wearing a winter coat and hat. A few minutes after that I met a man who worked as a monitor at one of the kiosks discussed below. He told me how excited he was to have a job. It paid about US$5 per week.

When representatives of the Rotary Club of Denver SE visited Silanga in 2006, they were struck by the harsh environment. Unemployment, inadequate nutrition, inefficient services and infrastructure, weak governance, and basic impoverishment stood out. So did issues surrounding water and sanitation. In discussion with Silanga residents, Kenyan Rotarians, and representatives of a United Kingdom-based group called Practical Action, under the initial leadership of a Denver Rotarian named Mike Klingbiel a "plan of attack" was developed.

A grant of $330,000 was secured from Rotary International. Designs were created such that eight cement-block kiosks or stations could be constructed in Silanga, a first-of-their-kind there. Whether split-level or single-story, each would eventually contain separate men's and women's showers, flushing toilets, sinks, and external water storage tanks. Each would have paid monitors; privacy (a human rights concern) would be respected. The storage tanks would provide water not only for the facilities but for purchase by community members for use at home. As Renée Botta, one of the project's coleaders, noted, suggestions from the community were incorporated from the start. Hygiene training became key, as behavioral change became key. Space was created near each kiosk to accommodate other income-generating activities, such as water purification services and sale of household commodities (Loeb and Botta 2011).

Open sewers like this one run through the alleys of Silanga, one of Kibera's villages.

Early on, an informal group called the Kibera

Working Group was formed to assist with project development, cross-cultural liaison activity, fund-raising, monitoring, advising, and applied research. It was led by Rotarians and University of Denver faculty with expertise in fund-raising, health communications, business and entre-preneurial development, and African community development. Throughout, it was assisted by others, including Kenyan and American university students. It developed and maintained cooperative, affiliate relations with the Nairobi-based water and sanitation organizations Maji na Ufanisi and Ecotact, as well as with the Langata Rotary Club of Nairobi.

Although a formal needs assessment had not been conducted in Silanga prior to the start of facility construction, informal conversations and observations made it clear that water and sanitation challenges were extreme. The infamous "flying toilets" of Kibera were discovered, consisting of bags filled with human feces thrown out of a house, over a wall, and into an alley, usually at night. These homes had no latrines and certainly no toilets. The material remained where adults walk and children play. Open defecation still was practiced by some children (Raymond 2013). Throughout Silanga, there were few regular standpipes and latrines.

Local leaders said they would support what applied anthropologists call "facilitative development": Under local advisement, outside expertise in WASH (water, sanitation, hygiene) and outside funding would be welcomed. Soon thereafter, it also became apparent that outside expertise in business development also would be welcomed. As the construction of the eight kiosks was completed, and as the Kibera Working Group gained traction, "facilitative development" became "capacity building." This meant more than support from the Nairobi City Water and Sewage Company, from Rotary, from universities, or from aid agencies. It meant full-blown community buy-in and local institutional strengthening—which proved to be difficult.

On-site data collected by university students and faculty clarified constraints and incentives for ultimate project success. Constraints included perceptions that dirt causes diarrhea, that women would be attacked at night on the way to using the kiosks, and that human rights do not include water rights. Success came to be defined not merely by kiosk functionality (e.g., a faucet that consistently operates) but by community engagement (e.g., an indigenous community-based organization [CBO] that consistently operates the facility). A three-pronged model unfolded with sustainable operations and improved health becoming dependent on these factors: (1) hygiene, including community-attuned training regarding proper hand washing; (2) governance, including engaged CBOs at each kiosk; and (3) business planning, including innovative entrepreneurial activity and training in records management. Soap production and sales involving local women became essential. Children's roles also were emphasized. To quote another of the project coleaders, Karen Loeb: "The more people care about hygiene, the more women make money selling liquid soap, water purification, and other related items, the more money the [kiosk-associated] franchise makes as a cut from those businesses" (Loeb and Botta 2011). The entrepreneurial approach evolved into profit-making, social-franchising opportunities for Kiberans.

A framework was established that treats these facilities formally like pay-per-use businesses, creating incentives, implementing standardized financial practices, and instituting oversight procedures. Revenue streams were created based on use and auxiliary entrepreneurial activities. Facilities became franchises. What once might have been called "community wat/san stations" became "community WASH and business hubs." To support these innovations, a collaborative association of CBOs was started. A program called Global WASHES emerged. An innovative group founded by Kenyans, called Power of Hope, is a successful spin-off.

CHAMPION   Jockin Arputham

Jockin Arputham is founder of, and champion for, Slum Dwellers International. Founded in 1996, this dynamic advocacy organization now has chapters in 34 countries, spanning Asia to Africa to Latin America. But India is its home country and Mumbai its home city. Most of Arputham's efforts are devoted to the marginalized people who live here.

Under his leadership, sanitation, electricity, and permanent shelter all are pursued by this charitable agency. But special attention is paid to sanitation and toilets, because as Arputham has said, sanitation is especially tough to tackle, and a toilet affords a person dignity. Few of the homes in Mumbai's slums even have their own outdoor latrines, and none have modern indoor toilets. Slum Dwellers International installs public toilets, with user fees being charged.

As one correspondent put it, Arputham uses "non-violent guerrilla tactics" to accomplish his objectives (PBS 2015). He creatively balances the three types of resources noted in chapter 1: human skills, networking, funding. He rarely takes "no" for an answer yet is usually successful in his collaborative efforts with other NGOs and government agencies. He works especially closely with women of all ages. They become the organization's human rights advocates, community operatives, and spokespersons. By stressing savings collectives, enough funds are raised by the women to assist both individual families and community development initiatives.

The award-winning 2008 film, *Slumdog Millionaire,* portrays the gritty life of Mumbai's slum residents. As one of their own ascends, the residents' overall persistence and resilience prove paramount. Jockin Arputham fits right in. At the age of 68, he is considered a towering community figure, even though he stands barely five feet tall.

Along the way, there were broken pipes and broken promises; frequent repairs were needed and some early Kenyan champions did not follow through. Some CBOs faltered. This project has required internal/indigenous champions, external/expatriate champions, and clever approaches to incentivization, infrastructure maintenance, the engagement of CBOs, and interorganizational collaboration. What I might call "nudged self-sufficiency" has been required. The balance between inside and outside support/advice at times has been precarious. Water and sanitation improvements clearly have needed to be couched in a community context that features socioeconomic, business understandings.

UNICEF takes an explicit human rights-based approach to its work with water resource development, featuring the needs and involvement of women and children (Stone 2015). The Kibera Working Group and Global WASHES take an implicit human rights-based approach to their work, also featuring women and children. Globally, there is nothing more important than consistently pursuing the provision rights of water and sanitation.

CASE #2: FOOD INSECURITY IN SOMALIA

Food, and thus food security, is a provision right, as the Tree of Rights illustrates. In a speech to global leaders at the Milan Expo on October 17, 2015, US Secretary of State John Kerry urged more ambitious approaches to food security in light of climate change and related political challenges. "We need every country on the same page," he said (Reuters 2015). To be food secure means that all citizens, at all times, have access to enough food for an active, healthy life and do not live in hunger or with fear of starvation (USDA 2015). By definition, food security depends on several factors. Put simply, these are availability (i.e., the ability to produce food locally or obtain it reliably from external sources); access (i.e., the ability for citizens to secure and eat it, as needed); and quality (i.e., the nutritional content is adequate and the food is compatible with local standards/preferences). A situation of food insecurity can arise if just one of these three factors is severely compromised.

A curious confluence of political, social, and economic forces is at play in the eastern-most nation of the Horn of Africa, Somalia. Food security is almost continually being compromised for millions of its residents, and this case therefore serves as a bellwether for African human rights analysts. During the past decade alone in Somalia, all three factors noted above were variously compromised by a combination of drought (2011), political instability (ongoing), and commercial/market instability (2009–2012, especially). To understand food security/insecurity in Somalia is to understand, if imperfectly, the complex swirl of forces that influence residents' lives. There is no other country that I know of where this is so difficult to determine. The sociopolitical and socioeconomic backstory therefore must be outlined.

"Somalia is still considered one of the most dangerous places on the planet and certainly one of the least stable," according to a leading analyst, Shaul Shay (2014: 266), whose work is reflected throughout this section. From the overthrow of General Zaid Barre in 1991, when civil war erupted and clans began to run rampant; from the infamous "Blackhawk Down" incident of 1993, when the US military attempted to intervene; and from 1994 when warlords' "technicals" (i.e., jeeps ret- rofitted with machine guns, manned by irregular militia) roamed the streets of Mogadishu, the capital, with seeming impunity, the country has been "on the brink." During the 1990s and early 2000s, the central government was in tremendous flux; its effectiveness was minimal. In 2012 a bit of order emerged (but under a fundamentalist cloud). Exact totals are unavailable, but it is estimated that as many as one million Somalis have fled as refugees in the past 25 years. Somalia is consis- tently listed among the five lowest-ranking countries in the world's Failed States Index.

Yet in one sense, Somalis—and thus Somalia—reflect a homoge- neity, particularly linguistically and religiously. Although a majority of the approximately 25 million ethnic Somalis live in Somalia, many also live in Ethiopia, northeast Kenya, Djibouti, and in the vast dias- pora (which includes over one hundred thousand in the United States). Most are Sunni Muslim. Salafism, traditional Islam, and the Sufi order are also present, the latter in slight decline. Radical Jihadi Islam transects these. The sectarian tensions within Islam are being exacerbated by the food shortages described in this case. As Shay (2015: 3) stresses, this homogeneity is cross-cut by tribal, clan, and political party divisions: "Infinite rivalries [play out] against a back- ground of personal and sectarian power struggles." The impressive clan network spans, and engulfs, the country.

Clans are based on patrilineal descent. There are four main clans-*cum*-tribes, each historically associated with nomadic pastoral- ism: The Darood (the largest), the Hawiye (the most dominant in Mog- adishu), the Dir, and the Isaaq. Together, these comprise the Samaal, from which the word Somalia is derived. There are also two somewhat lesser clan families, the Digil and the Rahanwayn, each historically associated with agriculture. The pastoral–agricultural differential is extremely important and is associated not only with access to food resources but with access to power.

Each clan can be traced to a putative founding ancestor, a man often (and perhaps incorrectly) ascribed legendary status. Given the historical prowess and lineal affinities characterizing leaders in this system, it is no wonder that warlords have gained such power in Somalia. Warlords such as Mohamed Dheere, Sheikh Yusuf Mohamed Sayid, and the late Aden Hashi Ayro represent clans-*cum*-tribes. Highly territorial, they control the resources within defined—yet occasionally fluid—areas that can span hundreds of square miles. Clan elites and elders are adept at negotiating "hard truths"; compromise is often achieved by realigning loyalties, lineage by lineage. "Today my brother is your brother/ally, my cousin is your cousin/ally; tomorrow my brother is your brother/enemy, my cousin is your cousin/enemy." According to one senior Somali official, Sheikh Sharif Sheikh Ahmed, "All Somalis are armed" (Shay 2014: 47).

The segmentary lineage system accounts for this shifting array of loyalties. A clan is comprised of a number of lineages. "Segmentary" means that, when a threat is distant and external, all the lineages within the clan, and possibly those of other clans as well, band together to confront it. This occurred, for example, when Ethiopian troops invaded in 1982 and again, even more forcibly, in 2006. At the other extreme, when the threat is proximate and internal, one lineage within a clan will confront another. Alliances rapidly shift. This is what happens when one cattle herder challenges another, when a husband's lineage confronts a wife's lineage over a dowry, when a millet farmer seeks redress from a sorghum farmer. Food insecurity strains these relationships further.

Shrub land, bush land, and bare hills characterize much of rural Somalia. Rainfall is minimal, averaging less than 28 cm (12 in) annually. Millet and sorghum are relatively drought resistant, and are grown widely. Barley also is cultivated, as are various legumes. Livestock, especially camels and cattle, are critically important, especially to the southern cultivators/nomads, the Digil and the Rahanwayn. They afford their owners both economic security and prestige. Goats and sheep are widespread; while valuable economically, they do not afford prestige. Historically trade was dependent on camel caravans, and even in recent decades the encroachment of camel-herding nomads on others' lands has led to localized warfare. The search for pastures and water is never ending. (I saw these same tensions in west Sudan, when I was there in 1979/1980.)

As many as three million head of cattle can pass through a single Somali port in a year (Shay 2014: 45). The nearby Gulf States receive a majority of the livestock exported. The control of revenues generated at the largest ports has passed, under duress, from one clan alliance to another on several occasions in recent years. Furthermore, Al-Shabaab likely has generated most of its revenues in recent years from custom tolls and taxes exacted upon just three Somali ports. Al-Shabaab also has demanded donkeys for transport, each valued at about US$200. A camel can fetch US$1000.

Al-Shabaab exemplifies the difficulties facing everyday citizens of Somalia. Through the eyes of its own leaders, it is seen as a Somali-based revolutionary organization intent on aiding the poorest of the poor. Through the eyes of external analysts, as well as the eyes of many Somalia parliamentarians, it is seen as a fundamentalist/terrorist organization bent on subverting "the greater Somali state" while also inflicting damage in neighboring northeast Kenya. It was founded in 2006, as a splinter/off-shoot of the ICU (discussed below). It has emphasized the recruitment of youth with a mantra that, in essence, states: "You are either with us or against us. If against us, your life is at risk." It has claimed ties to al-Qaeda and possibly to Boko Haram, in West Africa. Al-Shabaab has morphed in recent years, and now is by no means homogeneous. Members of one of its factions have killed members of another of its factions on multiple occasions.

Somalia and its neighbors, especially northeast Kenya, suffer from chronic insecurity owing to tensions within this complex political morass that includes al-Shabaab. Military insecurity and food insecurity go hand-in-hand. A raid by one clan upon another often targets cattle. Those bereft of resources flee. Somali refugees in northeast Kenyan camps alone number about 350,000. "Rampant criminality, inter-clan animosities and small-arms proliferation stretch policing" (ICG 2015: 1). Raids inland are paralleled by those on the coast, and these in turn are paralleled by those conducted by the hundreds of pirates who patrol the Gulf of Aden nearby. As of early 2015, about 300 people were being held hostage by pirates in this region. Asymmetrical warfare prevails.

"Sharia" is not monolithic. In Somalia, there are several kinds of Sharia law, each with its own court. By 1993 an Islamic Sharia court, using a more moderate kind of Sharia law, was arising in the country, aimed at establishing political continuity and legal authority. In the absence of a state-based army, each court established its own militia. Political improvements in fact were seen. The Islamic Court Union (ICU) arose from this foundation in 2006. (It later changed its name to the Somali Supreme Islamic Courts Council, SSICC.) Aimed at bringing a semblance of political unity to the nation as a whole, with this type of Sharia law serving as a guide, the ICU variously engaged warlords, merchants, parliamentarians, and militias. While proclaiming greater stability, several of these militias paradoxically jointly stated on July 3, 2006: "Terrorism is compulsory." That same day they went on to state, in the newspaper *Al Jihad*: "Terrorism, extremism and fundamentalism are part of Islam and good" (Shay 2014: 52). During the past decade, tensions between the ICU and the TFG (Transitional Federal Government) have boiled over. As but one example of these tensions, the ministry of fisheries and oceans, an important link in the food security chain, has struggled to keep its operations running.

Since 2006, the ICU has targeted the semiautonomous Somali regions of Puntland and Somaliland. After defeating Mogadishu's warlords, ICU's coffers were strengthened and its military reach expanded. By some estimates Somaliland—which proclaimed its independence in 1991, an act not recognized by the United Nations—is the most stable region in Somalia. Some of its localized food production programs are worth emulating. However, the diffusion of information about what is working is stymied by societal segmentation and political dysfunction.

Trading networks that engage Somalis and certain non-Somali business colleagues in the Horn of Africa are long-standing but fragile. Food import–export strategies fluctuate, with slim government assistance. With ports like Kismayo regularly affected by the machinations of powerful clan leaders and al-Shabaab, everyday citizens have little to rely on. Shops are not stocked regularly. Subsistence agriculture offers more for rural Somalis, yet few small farmers can access reliable credit to purchase supplemental seeds, fertilizers, and farming implements. Foreign assistance has been sizable, but fragmented. As Michael Smith (2012: 6) noted, at the extreme, Somalia moved in recent years from food aid to food extortion.

Since 2009, al-Qaeda has come to play an increasingly important role as a regional power broker (although as of 2015 its role had been diminished somewhat). Beginning in late 2012, al-Shabaab—its affiliate—did withdraw a bit, African Union troops gained ground, and commerce perked up. Yet some two million Somalis remained food insecure, this in part due to the lingering effects of the 2011 famine. "In 2011 a potent combination of conflict with extremist groups, failed governance, poor rainfall, and high food prices led to the worst famine worldwide in a quarter of a century. A report several years after the fact found that it was much more destructive than believed, killing 258,000 people, including 133,000 children under five" (Hance 2014: 1).

The United Nations sent a peacekeeping mission into Somalia in 2007. In addition to troops representing the African Union, Kenyan and Ethiopian troops have invaded Somalia in recent years. (In 2008, some called the recent Ethiopian invasion an "occupation.") These nations' primary aim was to diminish the terrorist threat posed by al-Shabaab and the presumed destabilizing influences of various coalitions of warlords. In counterpoint, it is possible that Eritrea was providing arms to al-Shabaab during this same period. Eritrea and Ethiopia are bitter enemies.

Alliance, allegiance, reprisal, realignment: This is the sociopolitical pattern that plays out in this chaotic landscape. That arms, many obtained illegally or "off market," are so prevalent makes the situation even more precarious. Dispute, uncertainty, famine, desolation: This is the pattern influencing food security. That agricultural/rural clans tend to have less power and influence than the others exacerbates this and leads to a fatalism on their part. To borrow and redirect a phrase from sociologist Robert Sampson, Somalis are battling "compounded deprivation" (Coates 2015: 78).

On a brighter note, the Istanbul Declaration of 2010 laid out a path for improvement. It was followed by Istanbul II in 2012, as well as the London Conference on Somalia. The Transitional Federal Government (now having morphed into the Somalia Federal Government) has garnered widespread international support through these initiatives. Livestock, fishery, and agricultural stabilization were mentioned in each instance. While food security is being addressed, everyday citizens await results.

CASE #3: WATER SCARCITY
AT CANYON DE CHELLY

Water seemingly has been scarce in the American Southwest throughout the last millennium. In the 13th century reduced rainfall likely contributed to the desertion of many pueblos and cliffside dwellings by the Anasazi. In the 16th century limited water in the Rio Grande region likely exacerbated tensions between Spaniards and Native Americans. In the 20th century water pacts involving several major watersheds and their diverse constituencies were created so that rapidly burgeoning urban populations in Utah, Arizona, New Mexico, and Colorado could prosper. Since the 16th century, these developments have been paralleled by the efforts of residents of the region's smallest and most remote settlements—Native American, Hispanic, Caucasian—to survive with limited water supplies. These people usually have had to operate "off the grid." Their provision right, water, has frequently been at risk.

Canyon de Chelly is located in northeast Arizona in the heart of the Navajo Reservation. The canyon is a National Park Service "property" yet is owned by the Navajo. The nearest town of any size, Window Rock, is over 50 miles away by road. I vividly remember my first image, as my wife Kathy and I hiked across the canyon 30 years ago: a vast riverine sand flat, with a stream ironically devoid of most of its water, bordered by tamarisk and cottonwood trees, surrounded by towering red cliffs. The sun was radiant, the sky was blue, the land was hot. A Navajo guide briefed us on the issue of water scarcity.

Among the most interesting pioneering anthropological studies of water scarcity on the reservation was that of James Downs (1965). He described a pastoral people dependent on a livestock economy. Noting a scattered population dependent on sheep, and to a lesser extent cattle and horses, he also noted that dry land crops such as corn, pumpkins, squash, watermelons, and beans were cultivated. Irrigation was minimal. In the best of times, precipitation was modest. In the worst of times, drought could literally leave swaths of landscape devoid of crops and forage. Concomitantly, social relations could be stressed and altered.

Not far from Canyon de Chelly, Downs determined the impact that drought could have on an "outfit" (i.e., extended Navajo family). Ideally livestock should have free access to water. Seasonal conditions vary widely. Overgrazing, particularly when water is scarce, causes "land stress" and necessitates greater pastoral movement across the landscape. The disappearance of water in a key dam during the drought of 1960–1961 caused intratribal strains as alternative social arrangements were pursued, livestock were rerouted, and funding options for alternative water sources considered. With plenty of water an outfit can host others in need and reciprocal relations can be strengthened; with lack of water these arrangements can dissipate, as they did then. Scarcity caused the outfit he studied to split and downsize.

Therefore, a lack of water can exacerbate existing weaknesses in social structure and kin relations. Even respected indigenous diviners can have little impact. The installation of a new pump, while helpful in obtaining water, also can cause friction, since households may need to move to gain access. A "cooperative competition," to quote Downs (1965: 1403), exists as limited resources are discussed, challenged, and allocated. Direct confrontation is eschewed by Navajo as a way to get things done; thus contacts with government officials often are avoided. Water and grazing, with the associated cooperation and movement necessary to "make them work," are key determinants to social relations.

Today, the situation in the Canyon de Chelly area is much the same. About 50 Navajo families live in the canyon itself, with others residing above the rim in scattered houses and hogans. Those in the canyon constitute a single chapter among the 110 chapters that comprise the 250,000-person Navajo Nation. Most families rely on horses, as well as automobiles and trucks, for transportation. Most use a windmill pump for watering their horses. Springs are scattered, and check dams are only moderately effective in catching rain runoff. Streams and ponds, primarily located above the canyon rim, are intermittent. Some people truck in their household water, traveling (at the extreme) nearly 100 miles round-trip.

Turning Points LLC is one of the organizations that works with the canyon's residents. Founded by Edith Samouillet de Gomez, it uses a psychosocial sustainability model to gradually build trust and then in turn moves toward a project sustainability model to target water resource development. She stresses that "we promote authenticity, genuineness and responsibility" as projects are undertaken, while incorporating "willingness, patience, and active listening," without rushing (2015). Within the Navajo Nation, people ask fewer questions but spend more time studying environmental conditions. They are sensitive to subtle changes, such as those Downs reported decades earlier. Outsiders intent on helping may be rebuffed unless personal introductions are used to open doors and genuine rapport is established. Paralleling a mantra of psychologist Carl Rogers, Samouillet de Gomez and her colleagues promote unconditional positive regard. They try "to transform the toughest problem into an opportunity" that engages the entire community. They try to optimize "cooperative competition."

The Navajo of Canyon de Chelly own all the water rights; no federal, state, or local government laws can override in this regard. Yet, to address tough issues like water scarcity, collaborative arrangements must be made among the Navajo Tribal Council and federal, state, and local agencies, plus organizations like Turning Points LLC. A package of mutually agreed-upon resources is necessary to effect change. As suggested by the Tree of Rights, a rights-related intervention should be value mediated. Turning Points LLC has done this, as mutual trust is kept front and center. An intervention also should be duty bound, as the Tree of Rights indicates, and the organization has done this. Navajo and non-Navajo partners see collaborative work toward the improvement of water resources as a duty, to be pursued patiently yet relentlessly. One future result might be the installation of solar-powered "water health centers."

WHAT'S BEING DONE

In January 1980, I found myself in a Land Rover, bouncing along a rutted track in Sudan's remote western savannah. My team and I were working on a water resource assessment project involving the Kababish people, among others, but ironically we ourselves were short of potable water. I thought about what Michael Asher had written in his remarkable book *A Desert Dies* (2012), originally published at that same time. He was there when I was there, chronicling how the Kababish cope with limited water supplies. He emphasized the power of personal restraint and group conservancy, such that even when parched, when water suddenly becomes available, one does not rush to drink it. One waits. One shares. Water is a provision right, but when scarce, it also is a privilege.

The World Food Programme in South Sudan

One of the planet's more successful rapid-response institutions is the World Food Programme (WFP). It takes starvation seriously. In the post–World War II era, it has expanded into one of the largest United Nations humanitarian operations. The World Food Program USA works in conjunction with it. (The latter was originally envisioned by President Dwight Eisenhower and most recently has earned a three-star rating from Charity Navigator.) The crisis in South Sudan exemplifies its efforts.

In South Sudan, the world's newest nation, the dream of transethnic unity envisioned through its referendum for independence in January 2011 has largely been shattered. In December 2010, I saw people lining up in Juba, now the capital, eagerly awaiting their turn to register for the vote. Members of the two largest ethnic groups, the Dinka and the Nuer, excitedly told me of their vision of political egalitarianism, progressive development, and human rights enhancement. Teachers and preachers told me they were convinced that old problems could be put aside and that a new nation, built on an "oil wealth engine" and modern parliamentary principles, could quickly emerge. However, it was not to be. Ongoing tensions with Sudan (from which it sprung) and reemergent tensions among Dinka and Nuer (as well as other groups such as the Shilluk) have led to a situation that—as of 2015—was described as full-fledged civil war, replete with horrendous atrocities committed by both sides (Santora 2015: 1).

Pa'gan Amum, outgoing secretary general of the Sudan People's Liberation Movement (SPLM), told me in December 2015 that approximately 99 percent of South Sudan's homes are without purified tap water; 70 percent of the citizens are without regular medical care throughout their lives; 50 percent of the children are never able to enter school; and 50 percent of the overall population is at-risk for food insecurity or starvation (personal communication). In addition, it should be noted that about one of every 50 mothers in South Sudan dies during childbirth (CMMB 2015).

The situation had begun rapidly deteriorating in January 2014. Many refugee camps subsequently opened. At places like Wau Shilluk and Malakal, the camps grew exponentially. Of the country's 11 million inhabitants, it is estimated that as many as 1.5 million have fled; hundreds of thousands of others have been temporarily displaced, including to swamplands. The WFP began food security operations there in early 2014. By mid-2015, it was estimated that nearly four million residents did not have sufficient food (Santora 2015: 5). The WFP strategy features "programmatic resiliency" and "assets identification." Targeted food delivery, combined with family vouchers and pragmatic training, without favoring any ethnic group, has allowed it to achieve some success. "Burden sharing," a principle of obligated action discussed in chapter 6, is heeded. Attention is paid not only to food quantity but to food quality, with sensitive consideration of nutritional benefits. But, with warehouses raided and delivery convoys under attack, systematic continuity of relief is very difficult to achieve.

Securing Somalia's Fisheries

Despite the history of livestock and agriculture as foundations of Somalia's food resources, it ironically is fisheries that have the opportunity to make the most favorable impact in the near future. As Glaser and colleagues (2015) report, the coastal waters of Somalia have the potential to support some of the world's most productive fisheries. However, the 1991 civil war, discussed earlier, reversed the course of modest gains that the fishing industry had made. Somali waters became besieged by foreigners. By 2013, foreign vessels were catching three times the amount that small-scale Somali fishermen were catching. Much of the foreign activity is off the books, and much of it (such as bottom trawling) is damaging to the marine environment. Illegal, unreported, and unregulated (IUU) fishing swelled to a point where even Somali pirates were attacking these vessels for protective, as well as pillaging, purposes.

The work of Secure Fisheries, backers of the above-cited report, is both innovative and imperative. It is innovative in that it provides the most comprehensive analysis of fisheries food security issues in this region in the past 30 years. The report is very specific. For example, it notes that whereas marine top predators (e.g., tuna and shark) currently are being harvested at maximum capacity, the catch of fishes such as sardines, anchovies, and certain bottom species could be expanded. With the total economic value of domestic fisheries estimated at about US$135 million annually, there is room for tremendous growth. It is imperative in that it complements the recommendations of recent conferences such as that in London (mentioned in Case #2, earlier in this chapter), and specifies what must be done to make Somali fisheries sustainable: (1) properly license foreign vessels; (2) develop better monitoring and surveillance; (3) increase data collection; (4) grow the domestic sector through investments in cold storage and infrastructure; (5) develop fisheries management plans; (6) stop foreign illegal fishing by enforcing sanctions against vessels; (7) improve data sharing by foreign navies with Somali officials; (8) inspect vessels suspected of fishing illegally as they unload in foreign ports; and (9) support regional agreements to end IUU fishing.

Improving Somali food security by targeting fisheries, as Glaser and colleagues (2015: iii) stress, could "bolster food and income security throughout the region. A more robust domestic fishery would increase jobs and wages in one of Somalia's most vulnerable employment sectors. [Pursued in parallel,] management of foreign fishing is important to ensure lasting benefits for Somalis." It also is important to ensure that this most basic of provision rights, food, is under Somali control.

> *"I have one last coconut. It's for you."*
> —impoverished Salvadoran farmer, to Peter Van Arsdale, 1984

Amum, Pa'gan. 2015. Personal communication with Secretary General of the Sudan People's Liberation Movement, December 15.

Asher, Michael. 2012 [orig. 1980]. *A Desert Dies.* New York: Master Publishing.

CMMB. 2015. Our results: Helping those most at risk. *Catholic Medical Mission Board*, brochure, New York, New York.

Coates, Ta-Nehisi. 2015. The black family in the age of mass incarceration. *The Atlantic* 316 (October 3): 60–84.

Downs, James F. 1965. The social consequences of a dry well. *American Anthropologist* 67(6): 1387–1416.

Glaser, Sarah M., Paige M. Roberts, Robert H. Mazurek, Kaija J. Hurlburt, and Liza Kane-Hartnett. 2015. *Securing Somali fisheries report.* Secure Fisheries: Advancing Sustainable Fisheries. Retrieved from http://www.securefisheries.org/report/securing-somali-fisheries

Hance, Jeremy. 2014. Poor rains then floods lead to food crisis in Somalia. *Mongabay,* November 11. Retrieved from http://news.mongabay.com/2014/11/poor-rains-then-floods-lead-to-food-crisis-in-somalia

ICG. 2015. Kenya's Somali north east: Devolution and security. *International Crisis Group, Africa Briefing No. 114* (November 17), Nairobi/Brussels.

Loeb, Karen and Renée Botta. 2011. Global water, sanitation and hygiene entrepreneurial solutions (Global WASHES). Unpublished manuscript, University of Denver, Denver, Colorado.

PBS. 2015 (Fred de Sam Lazaro, correspondent). Meet an advocate for the needs and dignity of the millions who live in India's slums. *PBS Newshour* (February 10). Retrieved from http://www.pbs.org/newshour/bb/meet-advocate-millions-live-indias-slums

Raymond, Nathan. 2013. Water and sanitation: Situational analysis of the WASH sector in Kenya. Unpublished manuscript, Josef Korbel School of International Studies, University of Denver, Denver, Colorado.

Reuters. 2015. John Kerry urges 'ambitious' climate change deal to ensure food security. *The Guardian,* October 17. Retrieved from http://www.theguardian.com/us-news/2015/oct/17/john-kerry-urges-climate-change-deal-milan-expo

Saldaña, Jenna. 2014. The sustained community work of El Porvenir. Presentation to the Rotary District 5450 Water and Sanitation Service Resource Committee, Broomfield, Colorado, November 3.

Samouillet de Gomez, Edith. 2015. Working effectively across borders at Canyon de Chelly, Arizona. Presentation to the Rotary District 5450 Water, Sanitation, and Flood Recovery Symposium, Lakewood, Colorado, February 14.

Santora, Marc. 2015. 'Senseless' war tears apart South Sudan. *International New York Times*, June 23, 1, 5.

Shay, Shaul. 2014. *Somalia in transition since 2006*. New Brunswick, NJ: Transaction Publishers.

Shea, Neil. 2015. Last rites for the Jade Sea? *National Geographic* 228 (August 2): 60–85.

Smith, Michael. 2012. Somalia: Pushing humanitarianism into the post-Pollyannaish era, and applying previous lessons learned today. *Collaborative Refugee and Rights Information Center, Humanitarian Briefs*, Josef Korbel School of International Studies, University of Denver. Retrieved from http://www.du.edu/korbel/crric/media/documents/michael_smith.pdf

Stone, Lacey. 2015. *Water, sanitation and hygiene (WASH): UNICEF's global commitment to water resources*. Brochure, United States Fund for UNICEF, New York.

United Nations. 2008. Slums: The good, the bad and the ugly. In *State of the world's cities, 2008/2009*. United Nations Human Settlements Programme. Geneva: United Nations Press.

USDA. 2015. Food security in the U.S. United States Department of Agriculture, Economic Research Service. Retrieved from http://www.ers.usda.gov/topics/food-nutrition-assistance/food-security-in-the-us.aspx

Chapter Three

Fragile Bonds
Societal Violence and Warfare

VIOLENCE IS PERSONAL

In 1974 I met a man in Indonesian New Guinea whom I will call Matamu. He was a headhunter. He was the leader of a remote band of 30 Citak warriors. My small team of explorers was likely the first outside group he had ever seen. His life consisted of peaceful episodes with his family, of hunting, fishing and gathering excursions, and of occasional episodes of systematized, ritualized violence. He always was armed with a bone dagger. Taking an enemy's head, while rare, was not deemed aberrant or atrocious. There was a place in Citak society for this.

In 1980 I met a man in Darfur, Sudan, whom I will call Ahmed. He was a millet farmer. He lived near a village called Rahad El Berdi. Our team was assessing rural water supplies and the possibility of expanding them. Ahmed was armed with a shotgun and a bag of shotgun shells. I asked why. He told me that cattle owned by Baggara nomads had been stomping on his already-meager crops and that— negotiations having failed—violence was next. Paraphrasing an expression from America's Wild West, he said: "I'm going to shoot first and ask questions later."

In 1984 I met a woman in El Salvador, whom I will call María. She lived in a town called Santa Tecla, just outside the nation's capital. Our USAID-sponsored team was assessing small-farm irrigation systems in the area. The civil war was raging at the time, and María

39

appeared terrified. I asked why. She said that her friend had been forced to take a trip to the Santa Tecla dump, to search for the remains of loved ones killed in recent battles—"the disappeared." If a hand or foot was protruding from the rubble, her friend would wonder: "Was it my uncle?" Like the *coselitos* (chunks) floating in bowls of Salvadoran soup, the *coselitos* of humans "floated" in the dump.

Violence is personal. While violent acts often target at-risk groups, it is individuals who suffer. While violent acts often support a cause, it is rarely the cause of the individual victim. While violent acts often are justified by politicians, they rarely are the ones killed. The rights of individuals—who usually are innocent—are compromised through violence. Their dignity, a key to the Tree of Rights, is violated.

CHAMPION   General Carter Ham

Retired US Army Chief of Staff General George Casey introduced me to General Carter Ham in 2013. At that time, General Ham (now also retired) was serving as the director of AFRICOM, the country's military command covering Africa. General Casey told me that he favors an interactive form of engagement where the senior-most civilian personnel go head-to-head with the senior-most military personnel as the toughest issues are tackled. He cited the 1950 conversations of President Harry Truman with General Douglas MacArthur as the postwar Japanese rebuilding began. He cited Ham as a contemporary example.

Carter Ham is sensitive to the "old war–new war" dichotomy. The old (i.e., traditional transnational) wars engage states, targeting armed combatants as the main victims; use large-scale conventional weaponry; are funded by government tax revenues. By contrast, the new (i.e., nonconventional asymmetrical) wars engage nonstate actors, including militias and contractors; target civilians as the main victims; use new and "guerrilla-innovated" technologies such as IEDs; are funded by governmental and nongovernmental sources, including plunder. Cyberwarfare also can be involved. Both "old" and "new" wars employ violence. Representing AFRICOM, Ham tried to meet with representatives of "the old" and "the new" whenever possible throughout Africa. As suggested by the Tree of Rights, he is first an adherent of debate and discourse. Charged with following the lead of the US Department of State, as the Department of Defense is mandated to do, he stressed improved troop training as a general security strategy for selected African nations, and improved open-source data acquisition as a specific security strategy for the United States itself. This benefits a unified command, and in the near future might even enable military personnel to engage insurgents through a kind of "expeditionary diplomacy." Ham believes the military should leave a "light footprint." Humanitarian sensitivities remain paramount. To paraphrase a comment he made to me: "We don't want to shoot people, we want to help people."

At the extreme, as the beheading videos produced and distributed by the Islamic State (ISIS) demonstrate, violence can be pornographic. Those searching for beheadings to watch on screen, even if not perpetrators themselves, are behaving in an obscene way (Hammons 2015).

In this chapter, I make a case linking personal violence to societal violence and, in turn, linking societal violence to nontraditional kinds of warfare. An "old war–new war dichotomy" has emerged. The three cases that follow are not representative of "traditional symmetrical transnational wars" but rather of what can be described as "nontraditional asymmetrical wars" (Van Arsdale and Smith 2010: 80–82). They exemplify a government-sponsored campaign of terror, an oppressive neocolonialistic militarism, and an insurgency, respectively. Each one has presented human rights advocates with hard choices.

CASE #1: ETHIOPIA'S RED TERROR[1]

Colonel Mengistu Haile-Mariam currently lives in exile in Harare, Zimbabwe. One of the few people to have interviewed him in recent years is the journalist Riccardo Orizio (2003). Now a seemingly peaceful man living in a well-guarded but modest home, from 1977 to 1991 he ruled Ethiopia with absolute authority and brutality. Believing that famed Emperor Haile Selassie, "the Lion of Judah," had grown out of touch with contemporary issues and grown apart from the Ethiopian people, as many others also had stated, he and a small cadre of military officers arrested the emperor in September of 1974. Some believe that Mengistu (Ethiopian custom dictates that a person's first name be used) later personally killed the emperor by smothering him beneath a pillow. Believing that a socialist state, modeled partially on that of the Soviet Union, would improve the country's economic malaise, Mengistu pursued a torturous path that ultimately failed. Along the way he became one of Africa's most tyrannical and violent leaders.

Orizio is one of those who believe that the widespread drought and famine of 1972–1973 opened the doors to the takeover by Mengistu. My perspective also takes this into account but seriously considers the longer-term degradation of the country's environment and its agricultural and political systems (Hailu et al. 1994; Van Arsdale 2006), much as in Darfur (see chapter 4). Whatever the beliefs regarding the early years of Mengistu's reign, it is clear that a Leninist/Marxist-style ideology was introduced, one that complemented the

---

[1] Portions of Cases #1 and #2 are adapted from my book, *Forced to Flee: Human Rights and Human Wrongs in Refugee Homelands* (2006).

ideology of the Soviet Union. The USSR eventually provided nearly $12 billion worth of military aid (Orizio 2003: 142).

Mengistu had solidified his control over the country by 1977. As his identification with and supplication to the "Soviet Reds" became stronger, he came to be called the "Red Negus." As emphasized here, the first portion of his reign came to be known as the "Red Terror," borrowing a term used decades earlier in the emergent Soviet Union. A revolution was underway. Throughout, as his so-called Dergue government implemented a diverse array of land reform and militaristic policies, he claimed to have the welfare of the Ethiopian people uppermost in mind, and indeed the welfare of other Africans as well. His cadre of 120 military officers agreed. He told Riccardo Orizio: "I helped and financed the ANC [African National Congress] when South Africa was still in the grip of apartheid. I was on their side when they needed me" (2003: 148). He claims to have turned to the Soviets only after the Americans and Chinese turned down his requests for assistance. He hoped that his overall strategy would make him a respected pan-African leader, while at the same time ridding Ethiopia of its "tribal and feudal past."

With Amharan, Oromian, Tigrayan, and other long-standing ethnic groups increasingly at odds, Mengistu played them off one another. As Mekuria Bulcha (1988: 70) so poignantly stated: "In the hands of the [Dergue] the revolution was skillfully converted into an expression of aggressive but covert Amhara nationalism. Covert, because it [was] expressed in the broader terms of *Ethiopia tikdem* (Ethiopia first) and *ennat ager weym mot* (Motherland or Death)." The notion of "Greater Ethiopia" was continuously played up, while in fact ethnic politics and the marginalization of ethnic groups predominated. As with Cambodia, covered in chapter 4, the emergent regime manipulated myth, tradition, and history to recast its strategies in a more favorable light.

Tigray and Eritrea (the latter then part of Ethiopia), as northern outlying provinces, were severely marginalized by the central government during this period. Resources were withheld. As administrative authority was centralized, the northern region experienced a reduction of capacity. That Tigray had come to be known as a leading center of intellectual enterprise and innovation fed the government's fervor.

The Red Terror spanned the years 1976 to 1978. It followed the first great famine of 1972–1973 and preceded the second great famine of 1984–1985. Its repercussions therefore were economic as well as political and extended long after. Estimates of the number killed by the government vary widely (cf. Hammond 2004: 34 and Orizio 2003: 151), but many thousands perished. Mass detentions, torture, and executions served as grisly hallmarks. Those people attempting to claim the bodies of their loved ones experienced a bizarre kind of extortion; they were required to pay a "ransom" equivalent to the cost of the bullets used in the family member's killing. In other nations in similar circumstances the phrase "culture of terror" has been used (Van Arsdale 2013). A "terror" indicates a move from arbitrarily oppressive and abusive tactics to systematically, institutionalized oppression and abuse; it is an ominous watermark (Applebaum 2003: 93). It exemplifies "spectacular violence," one type of structural violence (Nordstrom 2004). This aptly applies to what took place in Ethiopia.

The Red Terror was instituted as Mengistu tightened his grasp on the nation. Oppression was complemented by a "retooling" of key institutions. Former military generals were imprisoned or executed. The forced conscription of thousands of men from Tigray, Wollo, and Gondar provinces characterized one of its earliest and most ominous strategies and has been thoroughly analyzed by Bulcha (1988). The conscription euphemistically was called the "Peasant March on Eritrea." Just recuperating from the earlier drought and famine, which claimed some 200,000 lives overall, a large proportion of the conscripted men previously had been displaced and were just then attempting to rebuild their homes. Many were midway through their first planting season in several years. Being forced to leave these activities uncompleted effectively prolonged the drought's effects, even though adequate rains did fall in 1976 and 1977.

The march itself was intended to complement the military's efforts to bring the province of Eritrea back into line. Yet it was poorly organized and the peasant marchers poorly equipped. Their trucks were attacked well before reaching the front lines. Rather than face extinction, a massive and chaotic retreat ensued. Those who survived either made their way back home (begging for food and shelter as they went), gave themselves up to guerrilla forces (thus being imprisoned for up to a year), or joined the ranks of IDPs and refugees fleeing to Sudan (therefore abandoning their homes). Continuing a pattern of attempting to overwhelm its adversaries by sheer force of number, 1977 saw a similar massive conscriptive campaign by the Dergue among Oromo and other people of the south.

The loss of skilled manpower during the Red Terror, as militarization increased and nonmilitary industrial production decreased, created a vicious cycle. Conscriptive or corvée labor thus became another strategy of the Dergue. Although this practice had existed prior to their takeover, it worsened under their rule. State farms had been created in 1975 as a part of the nationalization of rural lands. Some operated on a "labor camp" model. Forced to leave family farms to work on these farms, with little or no recompense, peasants came to express avid resentment. The forced payment of "dues" further exacerbated the situation. This system extended well into the 1980s, with the farms running large losses owing to poor management and inadequate parts supplies. Rather than participate, many peasants fled as refugees (Bulcha 1988: 112–114).

Ethiopian elders in the village of Mai Misham discuss human rights issues in the context of community development.

The Red Terror was characterized by oppressive military tactics, unwarranted imprisonments and executions, and a forced restructuring of Ethiopian society. Abandoned schools and other facilities were turned into prisons, one of which—"Higher 15" in Addis Ababa, the capital—figures prominently later in this chapter. Funds were mismanaged and/or misdirected as the military was strengthened, in concert with Soviet assistance. Although taking place several years after the Red Terror ended, the self-congratulatory national celebrations of 1984 witnessed the same type of mismanagement and misdirection. These events recognized the regime's 10th year in power. The Dergue spent several million dollars on festivities, funds that could have been far better directed toward agricultural development during the 1984–1985 famine (see Bulcha 1988: 238). Tigrayan and Eritrean armed insurgencies served to heighten the Dergue's irritability at precisely this time.

Particularly terrifying for Ethiopia's residents was the fact that the Red Terror made individual vendettas possible. The newly elected *kebele* (urban residents' associations) guards, militia, and other security forces used their positions to justify and avenge old grudges. *Kebele* defense guards were primarily recruited from among the unemployed and uneducated. They targeted persons suspected of being "antirevolutionary." Uncoordinated, aggressive home searches and nonjudicial detentions were common. A large number of children were among those killed during this unofficial yet implicitly sanctioned campaign (Bulcha 1988: 102–104).

The Red Terror spurred interest and concern in the outside world. A number of authors penned fictional and factual works referencing it, as well as the array of events involving Mengistu's reign (Pankhurst 2004). Much as with Cambodia under Pol Pot, the Red Terror drove intellectuals and other skilled professionals into rural regions, which led to bolstering rebel forces who later overthrew Mengistu (Hammond 2004: 34). Guerrillas from Tigray were among those who succeeded in 1991, and one of their leaders—Meles Zenawi (now deceased)—eventually assumed the role of prime minister.

CASE #2: REFUGEES IN NEW GUINEA

Humans have inhabited the huge island of New Guinea for over 30,000 years. During the late Pleistocene, New Guinea and Australia were joined, with their populations possibly not differentiating much until about 10,000 years ago. These distinctions are important as modern Papuan peoples of New Guinea—the "cousins" of Australian Aboriginals—are considered. Their roots *in situ* are truly ancient and their traditions are grounded in extraordinarily rich cultural lifeways, only to be severely disrupted by explorers, traders, colonists, missionaries, and militarists from Europe and Indonesia, as well as other Southeast Asian countries, who exerted external pressures over the past 500 years. To understand what has happened to create Papuan refugees recently, under a neocolonialistic militarism with its associated forms of modern violence, the broader backstory is necessary.

The indigenous Papuan peoples were variously perceived by early European explorers (including Captain James Cook) and later Indonesian traders as "primitives" or "savages." In subsequent centuries their headhunting and cannibalism were used to support this view; they were characterized as extremely violent. The seemingly benign (but in fact demeaning) term *orang hutan,* meaning "jungle people," came to be widely applied to the Papuans of western (i.e., Indonesian) New Guinea by Javanese. Those of eastern New Guinea (i.e., now the nation of Papua New Guinea/PNG) were similarly characterized by Australians. Such perverse stereotypes served to further widen the gap between the more economically developed western and less economically developed eastern portions of Indonesia.

Along with the residents of East Timor, Papua's "savages" became Indonesia's "problem children" through much of the latter half of the 20th and into the 21st centuries. Former Indonesian presidents

Sukarno and Suharto saw Papua as a symbolic galvanizer for a frac-turing Indonesian state. Stated differently, it was being used as a pawn by multiple groups: Missionaries, traders, corporate entities, and government officials, who contributed to what Knauft (1994: 396) terms "colonial constructions." Little regard for the long-term welfare of its indigenous peoples was demonstrated. Adults were marginal-ized, children were forgotten. Labor recruitment, and occasional enslavement, of the Melanesian inhabitants further east was accompa-nied by the spread of guns, liquor, and disease. Much later, as I wit-nessed firsthand, an epidemic of influenza still could decimate a village and undermine its social structure. Chinese traders established footholds in Papua early on. In several instances they were the first to set up shops and establish trade routes into the remote interior.

Enclave development drove early underdevelopment in Papua. During the past five decades, processes of marginalization of indige-nous residents have increased as structural inequalities tied to cen-tralizing governmental policies have become further entrenched. Extreme fluctuations in the once-robust international oil market have contributed. Although offset to some extent by infusions of govern-ment developmental capital, influxes of tourist capital, and the cre-ation of cooperatives, which have enabled some Papuans to gain modest economic toeholds in the regional economy, these marginaliz-ing processes continue. Large-scale mining has created the biggest single problem.

Research conducted among the Muyu people indicate that some of Papua's earliest documented messianic "cargo cults" occurred in an area adjacent to the Indonesian/Papua New Guinea border (Schoorl 1978, 1976). This is important to the understanding of refugee dis-placements that have taken place in the same area much later. In 1953 a movement began under the leadership of a local prophet. Tying spir-itual entreaties to real-world material aspirations, a so-called "ghost school" of devotees developed. As the word spread, so did an outspoken animosity toward foreigners. As J. W. Schoorl (1976: 74) stressed, it was a "wide-spread Muyu belief that foreigners control unlimited sup-plies of merchandise and money" and that Christian influence, modi-fied magically, is important. I discovered the same pattern in a messianic movement of salvation that I studied among the Asmat peo-ple of Papua, Indonesia, in the early 1970s (Van Arsdale 2011).

Messianic movements—led by charismatic indigenous leaders, some proclaiming themselves as the messiah—try to right a complex, chaotic world order. In New Guinea they are interwoven with, or affected by, traditional spiritual beliefs, Christian missionization, mil-itary operations, guerrilla activities, and NGO-sponsored humanitar-ian work. In these "entangled worlds," to borrow a phrase from Eben Kirksey (2012), nothing is black-and-white. *Alam*, the natural and supernatural, intersect. Organisasi Papua Merdeka (OPM), the Papuan Freedom Organization, began in the late 1960s and at various times has been influenced by such messianic movements. Charismatic leaders like General Melkianus Awom, General Thadius Yogi, and my colleague Arnold Ap have arisen. Over the years OPM came to embrace a dozen similar organizations-*cum*-movements seeking freedom from Indonesian oppression. It came to be linked to a powerful yet amorphous Papuan nationalism, which bridges the PNG border. Claiming membership throughout both Papua and West Papua, Indonesia, it seems that its anonymous freedom fighters—like those earlier "ghost school" devotees—are "everywhere and nowhere" (Kirksey 2012: 181). The jungle provides cover.

During the past five decades, the Indonesian military has clamped down on what it perceives as Papuan radicals and their sympathizers. This pressure has been accompanied by paramilitary actions, usually taking place "off the grid." Asymmetrical warfare has become the norm; at times it literally has been guns against spears, soldiers against guerrillas. Under the coercive military leadership of Prabowo Subianto, the late President Suharto's son-in-law, strong-arm tactics were mounted. His paracommando initiatives in Papua against leading separatists and their supporters became increasingly oppressive and brutal. His father-in-law had solidified a "new order," and it was to be enforced (Van Arsdale 2006). According to reports I received in the field, on at least three occasions Indonesian fighter jets strafed the villages from which the movement's guerrilla leaders were operating. Fighting peaked during the 1970s and 1980s, when as O'Neill noted (1996: 11), several thousand Papuans were killed. Yet it has continued to the present day.

All of this is to say that thousands of Papuan IDPs and refugees have been created since the 1970s, and it was then that some began crossing the Papua/PNG border. OPM still operates near the border, as well as in other rural (and some urban) areas. Limited political gains have been realized in recent decades. For example, on December 1, 1999, the Papuan flag (originally designed in the 1960s) was allowed to be raised in the major governmental centers and towns. As the 21st century began, certain outspoken rebel leaders were allowed to have a limited voice by the Indonesian government. In sharp contrast, other rebel leaders maintained and expanded quasimilitary/anti-Indonesian encampments, where new recruits are trained. Although modern weapons are in short supply, they continue preparing to battle Kopassus, the ominous special forces of the Indonesian military (Kirksey 2012).

Refugees have been created among people whose grandfathers were headhunters. The UNHCR (2015) reported about 10,000 refugees and asylum seekers in PNG, most having traversed dense jungle and swamplands to get there. In part owing to the anti-Indonesian reactionary stances taken by the Muyu people for half a century near the Papua/PNG border, NGO- and UNHCR-sponsored programs have arisen near there, along the Fly River, which are conducive to assisting forcibly displaced people. Aid worker Abba Sorame (2016) reported to me via email that camps are found on the river's bank, as well as farther afield:

> Most fear Indonesian troops and take refuge along the river. I've interviewed one of the OPM rebels and he said [many experience] torture. He said that when Indonesian troops find out that one of the family members is involved with OPM, the troops will come to that village and torture the entire family, and the extended family too. . . . If an OPM member shoots an Indonesian soldier, it's a different story. They will mobilize all their forces, including war tanks and jet fighters, and double the number of troops to attack. . . . Sometimes a bounty is placed on a rebel's head.

Abba Sorame is currently running a financial literacy awareness program for refugees from Papua's Wamena region, also assisting them in opening savings accounts with microfinance incentives. A special objective is helping them save for their children's education. Some refugee women specifically list this as a reason for "crossing over," bringing their children, while also seeking informal marketing opportunities to fund daily needs. A number have set up small canteens. He reports that most of them feel safe when crossing into PNG. However, logistical problems are significant. Most of the encampments along the Fly River can only be reached by boat; there are few airstrips. Another problem is language. Few refugees speak English or pidgin, the lingua franca of the border region.

CASE #3: INDIA'S "UNKNOWN INSURGENCY"

While the tragedies associated with genocides were capturing headlines from 1975 to 2015, other equally important—yet more amorphous and more difficult to analyze—mass killings were escaping notice of much of the Western press. An important example is that involving Maoist militants in east-central India's Chhattisgarh State. As reported by Anthony Loyd (2015), this impoverished yet mineral-rich jungle region is home to so-called Naxalite rebels. They recruit from among Adivasi ("Aboriginals" or "tribals"). However, they also number middle-class students and Dalits (the so-called "untouchables") among their members. They patrol "a land of parallel authority, communism, people's courts, armed cadres, and IEDs." They state that their war began where the road ended (2015: 84). Some view their fighting as liberating; others view it as oppressive. Human rights ana-

lyts refer to it as an insurgency. Then-Prime Minister Manmohan
Singh termed the Naxalites India's biggest internal security threat,
with as many as 40,000 members in 20 of India's 28 states (Sharma
2013: 1; Wagner and Roussel 2013: 1). Residents of Tamilnadu State,
far to the southwest of Chhattisgarh, have been particularly concerned recently (Srinivasa 2015).

   The Naxalite mission involves a kind of militant communism. It
initially built on an abortive 1967 uprising of peasants against land-
lords, which had taken place in a West Bengal village called Naxal-
bari. Over the years, with the recruitment of a wide range of
disaffected Indians, so-called "terrorist coaching camps" have been
developed. Srinivasa (2015) claims that unwitting young people are
lured into the forest on "picnic tours," fed propaganda, and brain-

AGENCY ACTION
HRSP at the US Department of Justice

   Using a transitional justice template, the Human Rights and Special Prosecutions (HRSP) Section of the US Department of Justice's Criminal Division
was created in 2010. Drawing upon expertise in human rights, special investigations, and security, this new unit is responsible for enforcing federal criminal laws relating to serious human rights violations such as torture;
immigration-related offenses such as smuggling tied to transnational organized crime and human trafficking; and international violent crimes such as
those involving US contractors overseas. As suggested by the Tree of Rights,
efforts such as this, which use key resources, are empirical, and engage cross-
cultural discourse, can lead to justice. This happened with the Alemu Worku
case (reported in the "What's Being Done" section in this chapter), featuring
naturalization fraud as effectively addressed by this unit.

   HRSP investigates and prosecutes human rights violators. Homeland Security Investigations (HSI) and the Federal Bureau of Investigation (FBI) are the
primary law enforcement agencies with which HRSP cooperates in pursuing
cases. HRSP also is in regular contact with foreign governments, international
tribunals, and NGOs. Its work with the new interagency Atrocities Prevention
Board (APB) allows, as an HRSP brochure (2013) stresses, a "whole-of-govern-
ment" approach to incidents of mass atrocities and genocide. Even Nazi-era
perpetrators still can be prosecuted.

   Among cases recently pursued is one involving a former Guatemalan special forces officer, Jorge Sosa, who had been living in California. He was sentenced in February 2014 to 10 years in prison for covering up his involvement
in a 1982 massacre at Dos Erres, Guatemala. His US citizenship also was
revoked. More recently, several cases involving Bosnians now in the United
States have been opened. Some of this work has been made possible because
of HRSP's reliance on leads provided by citizens.

washed so that they will leave their families and join the revolution. It also is claimed that members of the Women's Liberation Force—some of whom are college students—have been attracted to the movement. As Loyd stresses, it is no coincidence that the war's epicenter is in a mineral-rich region containing coal, iron ore, limestone, dolomite, and bauxite, yet it is a region wherein some of India's poorest people live. In classic "core–periphery" exploitative fashion, mineral extraction has benefited those outside—not inside—this region. Central Coalfields Ltd., a subsidiary of a state-owned enterprise, "offered all sorts of compensation to the locals—jobs, money, resettlement, alternative housing—in return for their land and their departure" (Loyd 2015: 88). The Naxalites have been fighting back. The subsidiary's workers have been systematically targeted. The Naxalite base of operations is a shadowy place called Abujmarh, a "jungle within the jungle." Encounters with police and military authorities often have turned deadly. Firefights and targeted killings have claimed several thousand victims over two decades. Suspected informants have been bludgeoned to death with axes.

In an attack mounted in May 2013 about 200 Naxalite members—described as "Maoist rebels"—killed 24 people. Four state party officials were among those killed. An additional 37 were injured. Using a bomb and artillery fire, a convoy carrying ruling Congress party leaders and members was ambushed not far from Abujmarh. Sonia Gandhi, party president at the time, described it as a "dastardly attack" on the country's democratic values (Sharma 2013: 1). One of the dead was Mahendra Karma, a Congress party leader in Chhattisgarh State who had founded a local anti-Maoist militia. While his militia had made some gains, it also was accused of atrocities against "tribals."

Amidst this violence, it is difficult to distinguish which human rights are being respected and which are being violated. The police are viewed as the enemy. Adivasis are recruited into the Naxalite movement, yet both groups are extolled and abused. The insurgency needs funds. It relies heavily on mining levies, yet even more on protection rackets, profiteering, and kickbacks. Mines often are attacked because their owners have not paid protection money. Mine owners clearly also have rights, as do their miners. A Naxalite-run Jan Adalat ("people's court") allowed one family little leverage, or little say, before two members were beaten to death for purported violations. One man's eyelids were cut away with a knife. The family simply had been petitioning for the establishment of a local police station (Loyd 2015: 95). Other reports of butchery have surfaced as well (Srinivasa 2015).

To date, the Indian government has been incapable of devising an effective strategy to combat the Naxalites. Much like the Khmer Rouge of Cambodia, who claimed to be representing "the peasant,"

Naxalite leaders also claim to be representing "the peasant." The 1,200 policemen who have received commando training in recent years have done little to curtail or end the violence. The government's Special Task Force "is combing the forests" (Srinivasa 2015).

WHAT'S BEING DONE

Torture is a very personal kind of societal violence. It usually is state sponsored. On June 16, 2015, the US Senate reaffirmed a ban against torturing detainees at facilities like Guantanamo. Members voted 78–21 to approve an amendment strengthening US laws against torture. It also made the *US Army Field Manual on Intelligence Interrogations* the government-wide standard. This manual had been modified in light of incidents in Iraq and elsewhere. Where ramifications of warfare are involved, legally mandated changes—which themselves lead to institutionalized changes in behavior (i.e., reductions in violent actions)—can be effective.

The debate about Guantanamo led to broader discussions about war crimes during 2015. Labeling an unjust action a war crime is extraordinary. When ISIS destroyed ancient temples in the Syrian city of Palmyra in October 2015, it was labeled a war crime by members of UNESCO. Other human rights specialists labeled it cultural cleansing. When the US inadvertently attacked an MSF (Doctors Without Borders) clinic in Kunduz, Afghanistan, in October 2015, resulting in 22 deaths of staff and patients, it was labeled a war crime by representatives of MSF. When Sudan's President Omar al-Bashir's air force mounted yet another raid on defenseless residents of Sudan's Nuba Mountains in October 2015, it was labeled a war crime by American-based human rights activists. And these three events took place in just a single month. Events like this can be transformative. The use of the term "war crime" can galvanize a wide range of actions and, perhaps, can lead to improvements.

A Sensible Theory

To paraphrase the late humanistic psychologist Carl Rogers, "There's nothing so practical as a sensible theory." The theory of structural violence is extremely sensible and is being used widely to help address problems of violence. It also frames much of the approach taken in this book, as outlined in chapter 1. Monica Heller (2015) builds upon it. She stresses that deaths, disappearances, and displacements of the kinds discussed in this chapter are generated by dehumanizing processes. Structural violence allows difference to be made, such that destruction and appropriation can readily be engaged. Symbolic and physical violence enable one another. The state makes rules "to legitimize turning some people, their things and their land into available resources" (2015: 6). As noted in chapter 1, structural violence is not always physically violent, but it engages and legitimizes institutions that oppress. As discussed in this chapter, this applies to Ethiopia's Dergue, Indonesia's military forces, and India's Naxalites.

Complementing Heller's perspective, in my opinion, is that of Carolyn Nordstrom (2009). She introduces the phrase "global fractures." These represent lines of instability that radiate out from a crisis. Destruction and appropriation usually are accompanied by the pursuit of extralegal commodities and services. Arms dealings, illegal narcotics, and human trafficking are the three most lucrative illegal practices, involving perhaps a trillion dollars annually (Naím 2005, cited in Nordstrom 2009). Extralegal banking and mineral transactions also occur, at less financially damaging levels. Human rights violations occur along these "fracture zones." The accompanying violence is not always openly aggressive or bodily abusive, but it is institutionalized in such a way that it becomes insidious, demeaning, and dehumanizing. To quote Nordstrom (2009: 74), "multiple violences" emerge. For example, a war such as that in Afghanistan enables profiteering in medicines made available to casualties. Goods transported into the conflict zone are expropriated and diverted, by both the "good guys" (and their contractors) and the "bad guys" (and their tribal affiliates). Extralegal proceeds are funneled back to buy materiel, which often includes small arms and explosives. Food intended for the forcibly displaced is hijacked and resold. Youngsters are recruited to aid the effort.

Also complementing Heller's perspective, in my opinion, is that of Russell Crowe. The acclaimed Australian actor and director released the film *The Water Diviner* (2014). In it, he tackles the interplay of symbolic and physical violence through his interpretation of the aftermath of the Battle of Gallipoli, a defining conflict in World War I. British and Australian commanders had envisioned a "lightning strike campaign" against the Ottoman Empire, yet the fighting bogged down and eventually lasted nine months. Nearly half a million soldiers on both sides were killed or wounded. The suffering was tremendous. The Allies, and thus the Australians, eventually were soundly defeated in what was seen as Australia's first big symbolic test on the world stage. In the film, an Australian travels to Turkey after the battle to try to locate his three sons. As the plot unfolds, the film also allows the perspective of the victorious Turks to emerge. Said Crowe: "Growing up in Australia, you tend to see the battle from only one point of view. I wanted to have the audience [also see violence and its repercussions from the other side]" (quoted in Hammer 2015: 20). A film such as this can be very instructive for those activists trying to make sense of violence.

The Alemu Worku Case

Structural violence can have long-lasting impacts. It also can be tackled effectively by the legal system. The remarkable case of an Ethiopian man named Kefelgn Alemu Worku proves the point. As the US Department of Justice pointed out (HRSP 2014), when entering the United States as a refugee in 2004 Alemu Worku lied on immigration forms about his involvement in the abuse, torture, and murder of Ethiopians during the Red Terror of the mid-1970s. That is, he falsely responded "no" when asked: "Have you *ever* persecuted (either directly or indirectly) any person because of race, religion, national origin, membership in a particular social group, or political opinion?" He, in fact, had served as a guard at an ominous Addis Ababa prison known as "Kefetegna 15" ("Higher 15"), which had housed as many as 1,500 people. There he had engaged in the abuse of prisoners. Much later, he knowingly used the identity of another person, Habteab Berhe Temanu, to unlawfully obtain citizenship in the US while also falsely claiming that he was the father of five children. Alemu Worku's false statements as he applied for naturalization ultimately were his undoing. Testimony presented at his trial in the US District Court, held in Denver during October 2013, under Judge John Kane, led to his conviction on all counts. He was sentenced to the maximum possible, 22 years in federal prison (and stripped of his citizenship), for unlawful procurement of citizenship, making false statements on immigration documents, and identity theft. During the discovery process, it was noted that an Ethiopian federal high court had convicted him *in absentia* of genocide in November 2000.

Here is the backstory. A key trial witness, whom I later interviewed, stated that he had become a political prisoner in Ethiopia in 1978. He was sent to Higher 15 (from which he later escaped). He stated in court that he had seen Alemu Worku torture prisoners and that he had learned, indirectly, that other prisoners were being executed by Alemu Worku and other personnel. Two other refugees who now are naturalized US citizens supported this perspective during the trial. Kiflu Ketema, now a resident of Colorado, told Colorado Public Radio (2013): "Four of my co-workers and my friends died in that prison. I saw them walking with [Alemu Worku] and I saw gunshots, I heard gunshots. What does that mean?" After the Red Terror ended, and for years until Mengistu Haile-Mariam was ousted, Alemu Worku lived on in his homeland and then apparently as a refugee in Kenya. He then decided to enter the United States himself. Once approved, using his alias, he settled into a quiet life in the Denver area. He frequently went to the Cozy Café, a place frequented by other Ethiopian migrants. There, using the nickname "Tufa," he gained a reputation as a thoughtful man who occasionally offered advice to young people. He was "quick to burst into song, sit down at the piano or settle an argument when others had too much to drink. They welcomed his advice, his company and his jokes" (Finley and McGhee 2013: 1). One day in 2011 he was spotted by a fellow immigrant who recognized him from the prison.

The institutions, including "Higher 15" prison, which had been put in place by the Dergue before and during the Red Terror, allowed "spectacular violence," within the context of structural violence, to unfold unchecked. Another man whom I interviewed said that Alemu Worku had by no means been the only abusive guard and that he believed others also had migrated to the United States. Pulling out his iPhone, he showed me a photo of another man he suspected. "Those institutions were corrupt," he told me.

"Cure Violence"

One of the most unusual and innovative approaches to tackling violence is promoted by physician Gary Slutkin. Having spent much of his career fighting tuberculosis, AIDS, and cholera epidemics in Africa, he decided to turn his attention to gun violence in the United States. He came to realize that its spread is similar to that of an infectious disease and that, in turn, it might be possible to use strategies derived from public health and science to stop it. His initiative is called "Cure Violence."

As he shared interactively through a TEDMED conference presentation in 2013, Slutkin quickly realized—like many other researchers first addressing the issue—punishment is not an effective driver of behavioral change. Yet in the US and elsewhere, the problem of understanding and attacking violence was "stuck." The strategy had to be rethought. Using scientific (including epidemiological) methods, he began studying graphs, maps, and data sets from a number of American cities, looking for patterns. He found that violence in cities clusters, much like the clustering of an infectious disease. He found waves, as violence unfolds, ebbs and flows, over time. And he found that the greatest predictor of a case of violence is a preceding case of violence. He reflected on the epidemiological similarity: The greatest risk factor for getting tuberculosis is being associated with (i.e., being in contact with) a previous case of tuberculosis.

Violence therefore behaves much like a contagious disease. Slutkin surmised that the best way to fight it involves three steps that parallel those used in fighting an infectious disease: (1) Interrupt the transmission cycle; detect and find first cases. (For violence, identify street persons who are central and who can be trained.) (2) Find who else has been exposed but may not be spreading the disease yet. (For violence, identify those in the neighborhood who may just be hanging out but in the same group, and who can be "managed.") (3) Begin shifting norms via community activities, remodeling structures, and public education, leading to group immunity, as was done successfully, for example, in Uganda for the AIDS epidemic. (For violence, use the same norm-shifting approach within neighborhoods.)

Beginning in Chicago's West Garfield neighborhood in 2000, "violence interrupters" were identified and hired. Credibility, trust, and access were their street credentials. They were trained in persuasion, cooling people down, buying time, and reframing situations. Outreach workers also were identified and hired. West Garfield experienced a 67 percent drop in shootings and killings. Slutkin reports that this since has been replicated many times, in many places, with 30–50 percent drops in shootings and 40–70 percent drops in killings.

Another useful theory has emerged: Urban violence behaves like a contagious disease, and using a disease-control approach, it can be substantially reduced. While it would be difficult to apply this to the violence associated with asymmetrical warfare, in the near future it might be possible to merge certain of Slutkin's notions with certain of Nordstrom's notions of "global fractures." Cross-referencing the Tree of Rights, it is clear that creative discourse and debate will be crucial as human rights advocates move this process forward.

"Leaders with strong values build strong organizations."
—US Army Chief of Staff (retired), General George Casey

Applebaum, Anne. 2003. *Gulag: A history*. New York: Doubleday.

Bulcha, Mekuria. 1988. *Flight and integration: Causes of mass exodus from Ethiopia and problems of integration in the Sudan*. Uppsala: Scandinavian Institute of African Studies.

Colorado Public Radio (Andrea Dukakis, correspondent). 2013. Trial of Ethiopian immigrant highlights country's dark past (October 16). Retrieved from http://www.cpr.org/news/story/trial-ethiopian-immigrant-highlights-countrys-dark-past

Finley, Bruce and Tom McGhee. 2013. How an Ethiopian torturer hid in Denver for 7 years in plain sight. *The Denver Post,* October 20. Retrieved from http://www.denverpost.com/news/local/ci_24347284/how-an-ethiopian-torturer-hid-in

Hailu, Tsegaye, Tsegay Wolde-Georgis, and Peter W. Van Arsdale. 1994. Resource depletion, famine and refugees in Tigray. In *African refugees: Development aid and repatriation*, ed. Howard Adelman and John Sorenson, pp. 21–41. Boulder, CO: Westview.

Hammer, Joshua. 2015. Russell Crowe takes a new look at an old battle. *Smithsonian Magazine* 46(1): 20.

Hammond, Laura C. 2004. *This place will become home: Refugee repatriation to Ethiopia*. Ithaca, NY: Cornell University Press.

Hammons, Christian S. 2015. Beheaded: An anthropology. *Anthropology News* 56(1/2): 9.

Heller, Monica. 2015. Histories and geographies of structural violence. *Anthropology News* 56(3/4): 6.

HRSP. 2014. Denver man who lied about war crimes he committed in Ethiopia in order to come to the United States and become a citizen sentenced to 22 years in federal prison (May 23). United States Department of Justice (United States Attorney's Office, District of Colorado). Retrieved from https://www.justice.gov/usao-co/pr/denver-man-who-lied-about-war-crimes-he-committed-ethiopia-order-come-united-states-and

HRSP. 2013. *Human Rights and Special Prosecutions Section* (brochure). Washington, DC: U.S. Department of Justice, Criminal Division.

Kirksey, Eben. 2012. *Freedom in entangled worlds: West Papua and the architecture of global power*. Durham, NC: Duke University Press.

Knauft, Bruce M. 1994. Foucault meets south New Guinea: Knowledge, power, sexuality. *Ethos* 22(4): 391–438.

Loyd, Anthony. 2015. How coal fuels India's insurgency. *National Geographic* 227(4): 76–95.

Nordstrom, Carolyn. 2009. Global fractures. In *An anthropology of war: Views from the frontline*, ed. Alisse Waterston, pp. 71–86. New York: Berghahn Books.

Nordstrom, Carolyn. 2004. *Shadows of war: Violence, power, and international profiteering in the twenty-first century*. Berkeley, CA: University of California Press.

O'Neill, Thomas. 1996. Irian Jaya: Indonesia's wild side. *National Geographic* 189(2): 2–33.

Orizio, Riccardo. 2003. *Talk of the devil: Encounters with seven dictators* (trans. Avril Bardoni). New York: Walker.

Pankhurst, Richard. 2004. Ethiopia as depicted in foreign creative literature: An historical analysis. *Africa Quarterly* 44(3): 57–78.

Schoorl, J. W. 1978. Salvation movements among the Muyu of Irian Jaya. *Irian: Bulletin of Irian Jaya Development* 7(1): 3–35.

Schoorl, J. W. 1976. Shell capitalism among the Muyu people. *Irian: Bulletin of Irian Jaya Development* 5(3): 3–78.

Sharma, Ashok. 2013. Suspected Maoist rebels kill 24: Indian officials outraged. *CNSNews.com,* May 26. Retrieved from http://www.cnsnews.com/news/article/suspected-rebels-kill-24-india-officials-outraged

Slutkin, Gary. 2013. Let's treat violence like an infectious disease. *TEDMED 2013*, April (interactive video and transcript). Retrieved from https://www.ted.com/talks/gary_slutkin_let_s_treat_violence_like_a_contagious_disease?language=en

Sorame, Abba. 2016. Personal email communications from Papua New Guinea refugee camps, January 10 *passim*.

Srinivasa, Chakrapani. 2015. *Naxalites in Indian jungles*. Kindle Books.

UNHCR. 2015. Papua New Guinea: UNHCR 2015 subregional operations profile—East Asia and the Pacific. *United Nations High Commissioner for Refugees Reports*. Retrieved from http://www.unhcr.org/pages/49e488e26.html

Van Arsdale, Peter W. 2013. The danger of "culture" and the value of sociocultural systems: Helping forcibly displaced populations move toward stability. In *Sociocultural systems: The next step in army cultural capability,* ed. Beret E. Strong, LisaRe Brooks, Michelle Ramsden Zbylut, and Linda Roan. Ft. Leavenworth, KS: Army Research Institute.

Van Arsdale, Peter W. 2011. Taught by Friedl: The power of millenarian movements as reflected in a New Guinea cargo cult. *The Applied Anthropologist* 31(2): 17–24.

Van Arsdale, Peter W. 2006. *Forced to flee: Human rights and human wrongs in refugee homelands.* Lanham, MD: Lexington Books.

Van Arsdale, Peter W. and Derrin R. Smith. 2010. *Humanitarians in hostile territory: Expeditionary diplomacy and aid outside the Green Zone.* Walnut Creek, CA: Left Coast Press.

Wagner, Daniel and Mikael Roussel. 2013. India's Naxalites remain a force to be reckoned with. *The World Post/Huffington Post,* July 25. Retrieved from http://www.huffingtonpost.com/daniel-wagner/indias-naxalites-remain-a_b_3655315.html

Chapter Four

Crimes against Humanity
Genocide, Ethnocide,
and Ethnic Cleansing

BEHIND NAZI LINES

In October of 1944 a paratrooper named Jack Taylor landed behind enemy lines near Vienna, Austria. He represented the US Office of Strategic Services (OSS). He was captured by Nazi soldiers and transferred to a then little-known site in Austria called Mauthausen. Among other duties as a POW, he was forced to help construct a crematoria oven. He survived the war and later reported on his secret paratroop mission, as well as on the horrors that took place at this site, at what came to be called the Dachau Mauthausen War Crimes Trial. Taylor was among the first Allied soldiers to bring details of the Holocaust death and concentration camps to full public light via testimony. As his testimony demonstrated, he was among the first outsiders to understand—and demonstrate—how gas (i.e., "euthanasia") chambers worked.

As we saw when my wife Kathy and I visited the site and gathered this information in 2013,[1] the crematoria ovens serve as a kind of memorial to those who were killed at Mauthausen and its "sister sites." Mauthausen was a central location, with satellite centers at Gusen and St. Georgen. In Austria alone the Nazis managed approximately 40 camps and holding centers. As one clerk reported, when

---

[1] This introductory information was obtained on-site at the Mauthausen–Gusen Memorial Museum, 2013.

59

later called to testify, Mauthausen's crew alone cremated 12,704 corpses from August 1944 through May 1945. This excluded many unregistered prisoners, who also were cremated. During this period, it is estimated that as many as 50,000 died in the greater Mauthausen area. "Death books" were kept by Nazi Schutzstaffel (SS) doctors who were required to record the causes of death and issue death certificates. The causes usually were fabricated.

Shortly before Mauthausen was liberated, SS troops—aided by prisoners—began erasing evidence of Nazi crimes. Execution facilities were repurposed; gas chambers were dismantled; key documents were destroyed. Some of the prison guards began behaving more nicely toward the prisoners; the "writing was on the wall," and they presumably hoped they would be spared death when war trials inevitably began. Inmates nonetheless were able to smuggle hundreds of important SS documents and photographs out of the camp. Some also were able to preserve their secret war diaries. Guards had not known, for example, that "model prisoners" Georg Havelka (from Prague), Ernst Martin (from Innsbruck), and Josef Ulbrecht (from Prague) had formed an effective prison underground. Documents they later shared were very helpful in the prosecutions that occurred. They were able to confirm reports that began leaking through the "exile press," as early as June 1942, that something tragic was unfolding.

Commemorative and memorial marchers representing more than 20 nations gathered at Mauthausen on May 12, 2013. Several of the oldest had been imprisoned there exactly 70 years earlier, in 1943 (photo by Kathy Van Arsdale).

Upon liberation, in May 1945, some of the former inmates attempted to form lynching gangs. The US Army quickly disarmed them. Soldiers focused first on prisoner nutrition and disease abatement. Bodies that had not been cremated had to be buried. Local Austrians were asked to help bury the dead—and they did. Nowadays, as my wife and I saw at a special commemorative event, those who died are variously memorialized collectively as "those murdered" (e.g., because of their ethnicity, because of their political status, because of their sexual orientation), or individually as "those martyred" (e.g., because of speaking out against fascism, because of saving someone else's life, because of standing up for Judaism). Some who died are represented simply as "the fallen."

The primary criminal proceedings involving Mauthausen personnel took place during the spring of 1946, with 61 people being indicted. Of these, many were executed upon completion of their trials. One was August Eigruber, a camp overseer, who was executed in Landsberg on May 28, 1947. Places of suffering at Mauthausen have been preserved as symbols, including the ominous "Stairway of Death" outside the main prison walls. I could sense the feet that had trudged up the stairway long before I climbed it.

CHAMPION   Helen Achol Abyei

Helen Abyei came to Colorado as a refugee from Sudan. Since her arrival, she earned a college degree, became a community leader, and emerged as a spokeswoman for East Africans at risk of forcible displacement, torture, and genocide. She is an expert on the conflict confronting Sudan and South Sudan, including residents of the Nuba Mountains, as are her son David Mayen (a former Sudanese parliamentarian) and her son-in-law Pa'gan Amum (a former South Sudanese government minister, subsequently reinstated). Amum was held in detention and—as he told me in December 2015—five times was able to escape assassination attempts. He has attempted to bridge the divide diplomatically among conflicting parties, but with little success until August 2015 when a fragile peace agreement was signed. It only held for a short time. While Amum was being detained, Abyei contacted US government officials (including the head of AFRICOM) on his behalf, and also provided them with key human rights–related details as the South Sudan crisis unfolded in 2014 and 2015. In June 2015 Amum was reinstated as secretary general of the Sudan People's Liberation Movement (SPLM), the country's ruling party. Abyei is ever-cheery and collegial but also unrelenting in her comments about the horrors of genocide. She is a frequent speaker at regional meetings and human rights events. She also is an accomplished poet, with essays featuring African rights issues. Dignity and justice, as suggested by the Tree of Rights, are among the themes she emphasizes.

The Holocaust led to the deaths of an estimated 11 million Jewish and non-Jewish people. It was genocide, defined in simplest terms as a purposeful and systematic campaign against populations or religious groups, with the intent being their partial or total eradication. Such horrific actions at times are accompanied by ethnocide or ethnic cleansing, aimed at cultural eradication. There is always a political motive. This chapter details three other major genocide events.

CASE #1: CAMBODIA'S KILLING FIELDS

As Barbara Coloroso (2007) deftly explains, genocide is intentional. It is an act against humanity. It is bullying to the extreme. It is an attempt to gain tremendous power at the expense of those who might stand in the way. It is ultimately evil. Still, while not fully being able to comprehend how it could occur, how one group of people could inflict it upon another, we must nonetheless do our best to analyze it.

The phrase "Cambodia's killing fields" seemingly came to symbolize all that was wrong with humanity in the 1970s. It certainly came to represent a genocide so devastating that nearly one-fourth of Cambodia's entire population of eight million were murdered, or died by disease or starvation, during the Khmer Rouge's 1975–1979 reign. In its systematic targeting of non-Khmer people, I believe it also represented ethnocide.

One survivor was a photojournalist named Dith Pran. After his escape, he coined the term "killing fields," to refer to the many rural locations where "undesirable" citizens were killed and their bodies discarded. The actor who portrayed Pran in the 1984 award-winning film *The Killing Fields* was a doctor named Haing Ngor, who also authored a book about his own experiences under the dictator Pol Pot (see chapter 1 of this text). His book, *Haing Ngor: A Cambodian Odyssey,* was published in 1987. When I interviewed Ngor in 1992, I asked him how he was able to so powerfully and poignantly portray Pran on screen; Ngor had never taken an acting lesson, yet he had won an Academy Award for best supporting actor. "The things that happened to Dith Pran also happened to me," he said. "I was reliving my own horrors of the killing fields on camera." Ngor had actually lived the kind of life and endured the kind of hardships he portrayed in the film. We see the wily behaviors he increasingly is forced to use to survive; we witness his skirmishes with death at the hands of Khmer Rouge militants; we view him stumbling over corpses dotting "the killing fields" as he tries to escape. Those who survive genocide must be creative, crafty, and resilient. Many of the details of his life are covered in chapter 1, herein, with my book being codedicated to him.

Both Cambodia's descent into genocide and its ultimate liberation were, ironically, indirectly correlated with both Vietnam and the United States, two nations that were at war from 1965 to 1975. In the early 1960s, North Vietnam began a takeover of South Vietnam. The aim was reunification under a communist umbrella. The US sent in combat troops to fend off the communists, and by 1968 the so-called "Vietnam War" was raging. Officially Cambodia was neutral, yet in fact sides were forming and political postures were emerging. Long-held grudges against the Vietnamese resurfaced; many Vietnamese were even living in Cambodia. North Vietnamese troops also were present. "Communists go home" became a common refrain of Khmer (i.e., Cambodian) citizens. By 1970, protest marches in large cities like Phnom Penh, the nation's capital, had turned to riots.

Nothing is what it seems in such situations, as Ngor (1987: 38–40) suggested. In Cambodia "saving face" is critical. What is seen from the outside often is not reflective of internal dynamics. The late Norodom Sihanouk (who a colleague of mine and friend of his called a gentle, well-meaning, peace-loving man), as former king and more recent elected leader, had maintained a precarious yet lengthy political balance between the so-called "dark-skinned Khmer majority" and "light-skinned Vietnamese and Chinese minorities." He tried to minimize the rumbling color politics. Yet, behind the scenes, strings were being pulled. When the riots broke out, reactions to both North Vietnamese and South Vietnamese were intense. Ethnic and political pressures were at work. One of Sihanouk's rivals, Lon Nol, mounted a successful coup. (Some claimed that the CIA assisted; some of Nol's faction claimed American allegiance.) With the father-figure Sihanouk having to flee and work out-of-country, in exile in China, his influence briefly waned. North Vietnamese attacks had also begun, in concert with the war transpiring to the east. American B-52s had begun bombing the countryside in response. Political, economic, and cultural upheaval was becoming severe; a void ripe for exploitation was opening.

These were harbingers of the greater turmoil to come. From this morass, and with Sihanouk lending initial support from afar, the Khmer Rouge emerged. China provided backing. As businessmen, businesswomen, bankers, doctors, and teachers were exhorted to adopt certain pro-Sihanouk or pro-Nol stances, behind-the-scenes manipulations were assuring that institutions—and these prominent individuals themselves—would be bent to the will of a new kind of leader. The Khmer Rouge invented "Angka." The revolution began with "Year Zero."

Claiming Angka as its guiding force, the Khmer Rouge defeated the Lon Nol government in 1975. As Welaratna (1993) stresses, little was known about Angka or the Khmer Rouge, other than they were ethnic Khmer. Many saw them as a new kind of communist, bent on boldly assisting the peasants (i.e., the "Old People"). Their leaders offered peace, nonalignment, and prosperity under an egalitarian umbrella based on agriculture. Initially, as has occurred in so many situations that devolved into genocide, "traditional social values" (couched within an ethnically pure frame) were proclaimed. Freedom from oppressors was proclaimed. Extraction from urban life, and from the ways of Western-influenced urbanites and professionals, was touted as the route to success. Such urbanites would be transformed into "New People," working in the fields.

In fact, as cities were evacuated, "New People" could better be described as "war slaves" (Ngor 1987: 202). The agricultural labor was torturous, and as the months went on, torture itself was inflicted. Nationwide, religion was abolished. Buddhist monks were condemned as people who sucked off the efforts of others. Some temples were turned into prisons. The traditional family was abolished. Individual possessions were abolished. All devotion was to be turned toward Angka, the mysterious and imperious overlord. Intellectuals were out; professionals (including doctors) were out; humanitarians were out. As one Khmer Rouge leader proclaimed, "How lucky you are! The young people don't even have to go to school! Under Angka, the 'school' is the farm. The 'fountain pen' is the plow. The 'paper' is the land. You can 'write' all you want. Everything is free" (Ngor 1987:198–199). Each person was to forcibly participate, in a small way, in the radical reorganization of Cambodian society. Each was to join "the struggle," to "cultivate rice fields vigorously," to "achieve victory over the elements," and, of course, to demonstrate "revolutionary zeal" (Ngor 1987: 197).

Early on, the Khmer Rouge murdered those who were perceived to be enemies of the revolution, including officials of the former government, educated and wealthy urbanites, monks, and Vietnamese. There was a process of ethnocide. Yet as Welaratna (1993: 96) stresses, as time went on the killings became indiscriminate. Even "Old People" were tortured and killed. The rice fields became killing fields. Regimented cadres of workers were, in some cases, literally worked to death. Those who deviated from the guidelines laid down by the mysterious Angka, which came to be embodied in the dictator Pol Pot, were tortured, imprisoned, or executed. Those who represented "the old elite" were eliminated. In fact, "harmonization" became "homogenization." "Difference" and "diversity" were replaced by a monolithic, social sameness.

Viewing themselves as liberators, and viewing themselves as victors in the recent war with America, emboldened Vietnamese soldiers entered Cambodia in force in 1979. A complex array of Khmer Rouge, Vietnamese, Chinese, and American political forces were at play, both inside and outside the country. The genocidal campaign lasted from 1975 through 1979. Some two million died. In what is an ironic footnote, the Vietnamese came to save Cambodia but—in a different way—caused as much upheaval as the Khmer Rouge. They were resented by most Cambodians. They used forced labor. They laid land mines. They engaged puppet leaders. The nation was renamed the People's Republic of Kampuchea.

Kum is the revenge of people, lingering beneath the surface but never forgotten. It is central to the Cambodian mind-set, many claim. *Kama* is the revenge of the gods, seeking ultimate justice when humans fail to do so. To his death, the dictator Pol Pot was unrepentant. At his death, Cambodians declared victories for *kum* and *kama*.

CASE #2: GENOCIDE IN DARFUR[2]

"The *janjaweed*'s acts aren't human. They're committing genocide in Darfur, absolutely." This statement was made to me by a Masalit tribesman from Darfur, Sudan. Having escaped a number of years ago and made his way to Denver as a refugee, he became an eloquent spokesman for those still struggling in western Sudan and Chad. A friend of this man, also a refugee from Darfur, told me what had happened to his college classmate. A bright student, she had excelled at college in the town of Nyala. When he fled, he lost track of her. Through a colleague, he later learned that she had become pregnant and a few months later had been captured by the horseback-mounted, government-backed raiders known as *janjaweed*. As an apparent "rite of passage," one *janjaweed* youth—earlier chastised for his lack of aggression—had chosen her as his victim. He killed her, slit open her belly, and removed her fetus. He then impaled it on a spear, to the acclaim of his fellow raiders. In another report, relayed to me by the same person, another woman whom he had known also had been killed in western Darfur. She was hastily buried by members of her family. The next day, in an attempt to further terrorize the village, several members of the *janjaweed* dug up her body and decapitated it.

Drought, famine, and civil war represent the interactive array of ecological, socioeconomic, and political factors at play in western Sudan. The leadership of Omar al-Bashir, president since 1993, has exacerbated the situation and led to the purposeful brutalization of his own citizens. Hundreds of thousands of refugees and IDPs have been created since 2003—not a new phenomenon in the region when viewed historically. Since then, perhaps 400,000 people have become casualties as a result of predations, social upheaval, and resource scarcities. Entire villages have been razed and burned; in some cases no one was

---

[2] Portions of this section are adapted from my paper, *Ethnicity as a Basis of Rebellion and Division in Darfur* (2008).

left alive. During the past 25 years, as many as two million Sudanese throughout the country have died under duress or been killed.

In Sudan as elsewhere, statewide systemic dysfunction can lead to rebellion, genocide, and possibly ethnocide. A consideration of ethnicity, as well as long-term resource exploitation strategies, is essential. The fluid nature of ethnicity also is emphasized by Gérard Prunier (2005), who authored the single most comprehensive historical analysis yet of the situation leading to the atrocities in Darfur. Since the founding of the Sultanate of Darfur in the 14th century, a swirl of independent political operations, combined with assimilationist practices, forced displacement, and slave raiding, created a region both rife with problems and rich in prospects. Processes of Islamization were penetrating, stabilizing, and nominally all-encompassing. Mahdist revitalization movements (which emerged most forcefully in the 19th century and were aimed at overthrowing outside rule) reaffirmed the importance of indigenous religious leaders. Famed British General Charles Gordon's military incursions were rebuffed, and he was killed in Sudan in 1885. Other incursions followed. Then in 1899, Britain and Egypt combined political forces, with subsequent colonial benign neglect under Anglo-Egyptian condominium rule contributing to the marginalization of the region. The neocolonial marginalizing practices even after Sudan gained independence in 1956 have continued to the present.

The Fur (indigenous, non-Arabic people in the region) are a prime example to illustrate both ethnic fluidity and cultural complexity. Since neither their language nor their religious practice can be used to readily categorize them, their pattern of livelihood becomes the *de facto* key to distinguishing them. Yet this is complicated. Many are farmers. Some are livestock herders. Some are both. Of those who maintain herds of cattle, some have been labeled as "Fur el Baggara" owing to their connections—putative and real—with "traditional" Baggara cattle Arabs, who themselves are not easy to categorize ethnically. For example, it is possible to meet a member of the Berti "tribe" who also is "Fur" and "Baggara." Adoption of a migrant into a group also occurs with relative ease. One's current community membership usually is deemed more important than one's ancestry. Indeed, the original Fur state was founded by its indigenous residents on the principle of ethnic assimilation (de Waal 2005: 48).

Scattered amidst these peoples are others who are immigrants or itinerant traders. I met truck drivers from Libya and livestock herders from Chad. Some cross the international border on a regular basis with papers; some cross on a regular basis without papers. The so-called "annual orbits" of herders can span hundreds of miles; several of the most well established cross the borders between Sudan, Chad, and Libya.

Deterioration of both crop and grazing lands has been occurring for decades in these areas. The relative paucity of potable water, in concert with polluted reservoir supplies, has been exacerbated by live-stock herd growth, which puts increasing pressure on water and graz-ing resources. Increased herd size is promoted by citizens as a buffer against the vagaries of drought and famine, as well as against the vagaries of Sudanese government policies. Famine is a political—and politicizing—process. While in one extremely important way it refers to the systematic lack of food and nourishment for a population, such that suffering and death might ensue, in another way it refers to a complex of political, ecological, and economic factors that impair a society. Impairment in Darfur certainly has taken place.

Into this fractious environment, Sudanese federal policies under Omar al-Bashir have muddied the waters. "Since 1985 Darfur had been a time-bomb waiting for a fuse," Gérard Prunier wrote in 2005 (p. 86). "All of central Africa is a hand grenade, its pin pulled by a history of resource exploitation," Bryan Christy wrote a decade later, in 2015 (p. 51). Darfur's basic problem is one of resources, compounded by an ineffectual and oppressive state political system, itself more reactive than proactive in dealing with resource constraints. As I witnessed 35 years ago, and as is still seen today, there is tremendous tension between the centralizing tendencies of the capital Khartoum's govern-ment and the decentralizing tendencies of the remote regions. A type of core–periphery relationship exists. Stated differently, it is not "a series of events" that are to blame, but rather, a dysfunctional system.

Yet extreme events like these are tied to human motivations and decisions, intimately linked to the system, and cannot be minimized or explained away. Human culpability must be emphasized. The culpabil-ity of al-Bashir must be emphasized, as the International Criminal Court (ICC) did in 2009, when it indicted him for crimes involving Dar-fur. Genocide and ethnocide both were stressed. ICC prosecutor Luis Moreno-Ocampo said: "He used the army, he enrolled the Militia/Janja-weed. They all report to him, they all obey him. His control is absolute" (quoted in Christy 2015: 56). That the ominous Abu Tira, the Central Reserve Police, also report to al-Bashir further emphasizes the problem.

In 2002 the Darfur Liberation Front was founded. It readily evolved into the Sudanese Liberation Army (SLA) and was comprised of representatives of several ethnic groups. The SLA's founding mani-festo included its vehement protests against the central government's "policies of marginalization, racial discrimination, exclusion, exploita-tion, and divisiveness." Its objective was "to create a united democratic Sudan on a new basis of equality, complete restructuring and devolu-tion of power [aimed at] political pluralism and moral and material prosperity for all Sudanese" (Power 2004: 62). Another organization, JEM (Justice and Equality Movement), subsequently arose and also claimed similar objectives on behalf of Darfur's residents. However, by 2007 infighting between these two groups, as well as problems arising among other factions, were straining citizens' abilities to combat the central government's abuses.

There have been raiders and bandits of various types in Sudan for centuries (Prunier 2005: 13). Sultans, colonialists, local leaders, and sheikhs all would use raiders, some of whom would operate quasi-independently and others of whom would operate as mercenaries. In Darfur in recent decades so-called Arab cattle raiders occasionally would sweep into a non-Arab village and abscond with a few head. The now-infamous *janjaweed* loosely trace their origins to such raiders, past and present. However, the tactics they employed beginning in 2003 also can be traced to the tactics used by the north in its battle with the south (now, the nation of South Sudan) over a 20-year period. Government-sponsored air attacks against Dinka and other ethnic groups in the south were complemented by ground attacks utilizing Arab raiders. Many likely were trained in militia camps during the 1990s. In Darfur, since 2010, the *janjaweed* likely have been recruiting from among Darfur's own Rizeigat tribe, further muddying the "ethnic waters." Thus the older north–south battle pattern within Sudan has been replicated, to some extent, in the newer east–west battle pattern.

Most of the *janjaweed* raiders initially were recruited from among the so-called "Arab nomads." Yet, as the above analysis indicates, this is by no means a clearly definable group. Early on, many of their activities were coordinated by Sheikh Musa Hilal, who was working directly for the central Sudanese government (Power 2004). The *janjaweed* under his command, albeit operating loosely, ransacked and burned villages, pillaged supplies, and raped large numbers of women. They enacted the genocide.

Recently, the crisis in Darfur has been further complicated by the activities of the Lord's Resistance Army (LRA), led by the elusive Joseph Kony. Since 2006, when he first left Uganda—his battle to overthrow its government derailed—and entered the Democratic Republic of Congo (DRC), he and a hard-core group of a few hundred fighters have evaded capture and continued to create havoc in the region encompassing northeast DRC, southwest South Sudan, east Central African Republic, and southwest Sudan (including Darfur). Elephant ivory has become the LRA's currency. Much of it likely is headed to East Asia. Predations in DRC's Garamba National Park and elsewhere have led to the slaughter of thousands of animals. It is claimed that poachers are given quotas and delivery deadlines by Kony. Many park rangers have been murdered. Members of the Sudanese and South Sudanese military have been co-opted, some even trading salt, sugar, and weapons for ivory (Christy 2015). The LRA's activities also are covered in the introduction and in chapter 5.

Clearly, then, the complex array of ethnic relations must be understood, but ethnicity does not *cause* genocide. Resource exploitation, in concert with ethnic discrimination and corrupt government practices—where a more powerful group seeks disproportionate advantage over a less powerful group—does. In Sudan, the diverse types of ethnic relations are exacerbated by, and interactive with, an ideology of Muslim religious and Arab racial superiority. A supremacist mandate, centered in Khartoum, has existed for decades. "Killing fields" recently have emerged in South Sudan, magnifying the overall regional problem (Kristof 2016). While resources are limited, they nonetheless are manipulated, and socioeconomic strategies are conceived that negatively impact those most in need. As this unfolds, those in the margins are dehumanized.

CASE #3:
BOSNIA'S OMARSKA CONCENTRATION CAMP[3]

As the history of Mauthausen during World War II clearly indicates, concentration and prison camps have come to be associated with genocide. Although not the case with Cambodia and Sudan, this certainly is the case with Bosnia. Camp-like prisons have a long history in the Balkans. They can be traced to the Ottoman era. For example, the local ruler Omer Paša often placed ordinary Bosnian citizens in such settings. By the mid-1800s his temporary military headquarters in the town of Travnik had, in effect, become "one enormous prison" (Glenny 1999: 80). While it was said that he wanted to assist the Christian population, his mercurial policies offered little of substance to either Muslims or Christians. People representing various ethnic and religious groups were severely mistreated during these incarcerations.

The first 35 years of the 20th century saw numerous aggressive campaigns against various peoples of the Balkans. Some of the campaigns were led by Balkan forces. Networks of concentration camps were not yet present. Evolving transnational fascist influences in mid-20th-century Europe led to the establishment of true concentration camps throughout the region. From Romania to Yugoslavia, from Wallachia to Krajina, camps with the still-ominous names of Sremska Mitrovica and Jasenovac were created. Fascist Utaše forces, in alignment with German Nazi forces, were responsible for many of the worst atrocities. The Utaše were renowned for their brutality. Croatian by nationality, the Utaše followed Nazi patterns in brutalizing, intimidating, and

---

[3] Portions of this section are adapted from my book, *Forced to Flee: Human Rights and Human Wrongs in Refugee Homelands* (2006).

killing their enemies. The Germans set the agenda in most of this region during World War II. The Bosnian capital, Sarajevo, for all practical purposes was under joint Ustaše–Wehrmacht control (Glenny 1999: 498). Some believe that the very term "ethnic cleansing" has its etymological and experiential roots in this era, in this part of the Balkans.

Of the concentration camps established throughout the region, Jasenovac was the most gruesome. A majority of Croatia's Gypsy population is thought to have perished there. As Glenny (1999: 501) notes, what happened in the nearby village of Gradina was even more gruesome. It served as the Jasenovac slaughterhouse, with "hammers . . . used to beat victims to death in night-long orgies of mass murder." Other camps were almost as cruel in their treatment—and use—of prisoners. For example, hundreds of typhus-infected internees from the Stara Gradiška camp were forcibly transported to another camp near Djakovo in order to spread the infection. At various times and in various ways, Serbs, Muslims, Jews, and Gypsies all were targeted. The resentment toward Croatian brutality was extreme and still is recalled with great emotion today. (Some see Serbian paramilitary Chetnik activities of the 1992–1995 Bosnian civil war period as ongoing retribution for past Croatian transgressions.)

Ironically foreshadowing the 1995 slaughter by Serbs of some 8,000 Muslim men and boys near the eastern Bosnian town of Srebrenica, where women and children were spared, combined Croat-German forces gunned down some 10,000 Jewish men near Belgrade during the first part of World War II. Regional Wehrmacht officials refused to execute the women and children on the grounds that this would be "dishonorable" (Glenny 1999: 502). The atrocity at Srebrenica has come to be called the "Srebrenica genocide." Detailed accounts of this genocide have been provided by others (e.g., Honig and Both 1996). My approach is complementary and builds upon the theory of structural violence. Nowhere does this theory's value become more evident than in a consideration of the concentration camps that Serbs developed during the civil war, the war that led to the Srebrenica genocide. No camp was more ominous than the one at Omarska.

Today there are few visible signs that one of the world's most notorious post–World War II concentration camps once existed in the hills east of Prijedor. A midsized industrial town, Prijedor is located in the extreme northwestern portion of the country, within Republika Srpska. Martin Bell, a veteran of the Bosnian civil war, described Prijedor as "the hometown of ethnic cleansing" (1996: 58). As my University of Denver colleague, Todd Waller, learned at about that same time, a number of Serb-instigated atrocities occurred here.

According to ABC News, early one May morning in 1992, residents of Prijedor looked out their windows in shock. One said, through an interpreter:

> A long line of Muslim people were passing under my kitchen window. They were being pushed along by Serbian soldiers. It reminded me of a bad dream. The soldiers were bearded and dirty. They were using guns and machine guns to force old men, women and children down the street. It was a horrible sight.

Shortly thereafter, during the single day of May 30th, it is estimated that more than one thousand Muslims and Croats were killed by Serbs in this city. Also at about this time, in a scene eerily reminiscent of World War II, it was reported by Muslims and Croats in the area that they had seen members of their communities packed into railway and cattle cars. "They saw people's faces and hands reaching out from within the slats of the cattle cars. They weren't given water. They weren't given food. There was [sic] no toilets" (Gutman 1993).

Roy Gutman of *Newsday* provided the above quote and was the first to report on the emerging problem of the Omarska camp. This was on August 2, 1992. Britain's International Television News (ITN) broadcast the first pictures from the camp on August 6. Ed Vulliamy was the first journalist to be admitted to Omarska that same week. Helsinki Watch's human rights investigators arrived at about the same time. As reported by Danner (1997: 55), Vulliamy and his colleagues saw men whose "bones of their elbows and wrists protrude like pieces of jagged stone from the pencil-thin stalks to which their arms have been reduced."

> In Omarska as in Auschwitz the masters created these walking corpses from healthy men by employing simple methods: withhold all but the barest nourishment, forcing the prisoners' bodies to waste away; impose upon them a ceaseless terror by subjecting them to unremitting physical cruelty; immerse them in degradation and death and decay, destroying all hope and obliterating the will to live. "We won't waste our bullets on them," [said] a guard. (quoted in Danner 1997: 55)

As information began to leak out of Omarska, aided by the fearless reporting of newsmen like Gutman and Vulliamy, it became clear that a concentration camp—in every sense of the word—was fully operative. Following the lead of researchers at the United States Holocaust Memorial Museum (2000), the term "extermination camp" also could aptly be applied. Muslims and Croats from Prijedor and elsewhere in northern Bosnia were being forcibly transported by rail and bus, incarcerated in the harshest of conditions, tortured, raped, and executed. A large shed had been converted into a kind of "human hen coop," in which hundreds—and possibly thousands—of men (and some women) were jammed. One prisoner told Vulliamy that lying down was impossible owing to the incredibly tight conditions. He said he counted about 700 packed immediately around him: "when they went insane, shuddering and screaming, they were taken out and shot" (quoted in Danner 1997: 55).

A Bosnian Muslim journalist got a very different view of Omarska. Rezak Hukanović was taken there from his home in Prijedor as a
prisoner and, after his release months later, wrote the gripping book
The Tenth Circle of Hell (1996). He witnessed firsthand that extermination was frequent. Virtually every prisoner was severely abused.
One man had his genitals and part of his buttocks cut off; he died
almost immediately. So many were brutally killed during the months
Hukanović was in the camp that he referred to the Serb guards as
"killing machines" (1996: 109). Bosnian Croats were not exempted
from the guards' wrath, as many also were tortured and murdered. He
recounts one man, tortured and then run through with a sword, who
was singled out because his mother was thought to have been associated with the Utaše a half century earlier.

Hukanović also sheds light on the issue of identity. He believes
that some Serbs were whipped to a frenzy by what he terms their "pipe
dream of a state" (1996: 102). The fiery Yugoslavian leader Slobodan
Milosević (whose first name roughly—and ironically—translates to
"freedom") was calling for a massive Serbian resurgence. His procla-
mations propelled much of the violence as he exacerbated the Bosnia
civil war. For the guards at Omarska, the perception of reunifying a
discordant place like Bosnia within a larger Serb-dominated state was
tantamount to reclaiming the homeland lost six centuries earlier to
the Turks on the plains of Kosovo. It was ironic, too, that some of the
war's horrors were promulgated by Bosnian Serb leader Dr. Radovan
Karadžić, himself trained as a psychiatrist. When in 1997 I interviewed one of his former colleagues at the hospital in Sarajevo where
he once had practiced, she confirmed his idiosyncratic and malevolent
disposition. "He mixed politics and psychiatry in the worst way," she
said. After years on the run, it was only in March 2016 that he at last
officially was confronted and found guilty of genocide and crimes
against humanity by a UN tribunal based in The Hague, Netherlands.

The efforts of the International Red Cross, in concert with the
United Nations and other organizations, led to the release of several
hundred of the Omarska prisoners while the war was still relatively
young. Hukanović was among them. Analyses, although initially timid,
of the situation in Bosnia by members of President George H. W. Bush's
administration in the early 1990s led to consideration of the possibility
that true genocide was occurring. Institutions had been corrupted,
power misused, and structural violence therefore instilled. As specified
in chapter 1, structural violence engages and legitimizes institutions
that oppress and that systematically disadvantage at-risk people.

Responding to international pressure, the camp was closed
shortly after the prisoner release. It is likely that many of the approximately 7,000 who had been held there then became refugees.

The war ended with the Dayton Agreement of November 1995. Yet the effects of genocide are endless. The suffering continues. Erosion of the landscape leads to the unexpected emergence of corpses long-buried. Forensic investigations also lead to the discovery of remains, some of which can be identified, often to the relief of long-waiting loved ones. Whenever possible, remains are thoughtfully reinterred. Memorial commemorations are held on a regular basis at a number of locations; several of my University of Denver students have attended over the years. As Ed Vulliamy (2015) reported when he returned to Omarska, Ibrahim Ferhatić was the lone survivor of a day in 1992 when 125 prisoners had been dumped into a ravine. Ferhatić told the tale, therefore helping others better understand years later. On August 6, 2015, a convoy comprised of hundreds of cars wound its way through the hills to the Omarska camp site. It has now been restored to its role as an iron ore mine. Although not this time, visiting survivors in recent years had been allowed to visit the very rooms in which they had been held. On this occasion, flowers were attached to the doorknobs of rooms where women had been serially raped. Survivors and others gathered on the tarmac where Rezak Hukanović had witnessed some of the beatings and murders he described in his book.

AGENCY ACTION   Colorado Coalition for Genocide Awareness and Action

Community activist Roz Duman founded the Colorado Coalition for Genocide Awareness and Action (CCGAA), a nonprofit organization, in 2006. Its mission statement is straightforward: "To challenge our society to end complacency toward, and raise awareness of, genocides past and present, and take action to stop genocides today and tomorrow." CCGAA wrestles with the issues in academic, community, religious, and political settings. Value-mediated rights awareness and duty-bound advocacy, both suggested by the Tree of Rights, are balanced. When necessary, the organization leverages its modest resources to partner with other, like-minded organizations such as the Anti-Defamation League, Facing History and Ourselves, and the Peace Jam Foundation. Contacts are made with legislators in Colorado and Washington, DC. Conferences, lectures, and exhibits have included "Taking a Stand: Youth Against Genocide," "Genocide and Slavery: The Roots of Social Death for Economic Gain," "Deadweight of Complacency," and "Father Patrick DesBois: Understanding the Hidden Holocaust." While problems in East Africa recently have been emphasized, the organization's emphasis is worldwide. As Duman told me, antigenocide advocates must be tireless and unrelenting: "It's amazing how quickly we can forget these atrocities, especially when most occur far from our homes, seemingly out-of-sight."

White balloons were released, each bearing the name of an Omarska victim. Women held a banner that proclaimed: "Silence is Complicity."

> *"Dehumanization causes genocide. It's words, not machines, that create an Auschwitz."*
> —Rev. Gary Mason, East Belfast (Ireland) Mission, 2016

WHAT'S BEING DONE

A rights-related intervention should be value mediated and emotion sensitive, as indicated by the Tree of Rights. An unusual twist has been taken by the producers of Ballet Austin. Their presentation, *Light / The Holocaust and Humanity Project,* recently attempted to help audience members cope with genocide. Anguish, pain, and hope all were demonstrated through dance. The last scene was entitled "Ashes." The ballet's success has allowed it to be performed in other venues as well.

With genocide, the most important values are sanctity and preservation of life. One of the many challenges antigenocide activists encounter is apathy among those distant, both geographically and culturally, from the horror. "It's happening there," "We can do little from here," "It couldn't possibly happen to us," are common refrains. Value mediation must be accompanied by duty-bound efforts that are tireless, by those near and far. As the final chapter stresses, those who are well positioned resource-wise have an obligation to help those most at risk. "Obligation" is not "optional." Persistence must be absolute. An antigenocide mantra such as "Never Again!" becomes hollow if it is not accompanied by relentless activism and timely intervention.

Reengaging Cambodia

The Tree of Rights also emphasizes the importance of discourse and debate. In 2006, while serving as the US assistant secretary of state for East Asian and Pacific affairs, Christopher Hill engaged Hun Sen, an ominous former guerrilla commander of Cambodia's Khmer Rouge, who in 1985 had become the country's prime minister. As Hill (2014: 264–266) has written: "The killing fields had long ago returned to rice cultivation and Cambodia had become a developing country, struggling to improve its economy, manage weak institutions that often produced more corruption than services, and endure a political system that concentrated power in the hands of one leader." Hun Sen had recently imprisoned several leaders of the country's human rights movement but, when questioned about this by Hill, claimed that there was nothing he could do. "Our country has an independent judiciary. They are in the judiciary process. . . . Cambodia is very proud of our independent judiciary system," Sen told him.

Seizing a surprising opportunity, Hill recalled that—by coincidence—he and Sen had been born in the same year and month, and—upon asking Sen—found that he was 12 days Sen's senior. This status as *bong* (immediate elder) gave Hill the leverage he needed. He then said: "I am worried that if this [imprisonment] continues, Cambodia is going to have a reputation like Burma's. And what that will mean is that the [US–Cambodian] relationship will become very complicated. Mr. Prime Minister, I like to keep things simple." Sen conferred with his advisors and released the prisoners that same afternoon, while reiterating to Hill that "you didn't pressure me." Much later, in March 2015, in a discussion with several of us as he reflected on this event, Hill told us that the key to diplomacy, especially when human rights are concerned, is about "opening doors and keeping them open. It's not about telling abusers what to do." Hill also demonstrated a keen understanding of a Cambodian "saving face."

Reengaging Darfur

As noted above, human rights emerge through discourse and debate. They are experiential. They must be viewed systemically. As exemplified by the case of Darfur, long-term socioeconomic development, political change, and humanitarian outreach must go hand in hand and must accompany human rights initiatives. Land rights are key. To rebuild and reenergize the desolate landscape, sustained agricultural growth, complemented by "integrated" livestock programs (with some reduction in herd sizes), is essential. Careful attention must be paid to the voices—and thus the ideas—of everyday farmers and herders. It is not the elimination of the *janjaweed* that holds the key to Darfur's future, although atrocities must cease. It is not the elimination of famine, drought, and desertification. It is not permutations in ethnic identity. Rather, it is these citizens' own efforts at enhancing security, effecting a rights-oriented civil society that embraces decentralized governance and community-based development, and depoliticizing of socioeconomic relations—with the cessation of abuse. President Omar al-Bashir must leave office. The advice of former political leaders, such as Sadiq al-Mahdi (whom I discussed this with several years ago), must be heeded. As a former prime minister, he is widely regarded as a sensible man with a passion for justice. He told me that he remained cautiously optimistic about his homeland. As the Tree of Rights stresses, justice is an ultimate objective. Diplomats, local government officials (past and present), academicians, and everyday people can, and must, work together to achieve this.

"We must have eyes to see. We care for the common good."
—Steven Garber, 2015

ABC News. 1994. (Peter Jennings, correspondent.) While America watched: The Bosnia tragedy (March 30). http://www.mark.danner.com/interviews (accessed 2/10/05).

Bell, Martin. 1996. *In harm's way.* London: Penguin Books.

Christy, Bryan. 2015. Tracking ivory. *National Geographic* 228(3): 30–59.

Coloroso, Barbara. 2007. *Extraordinary evil: A brief history of genocide.* Toronto: Penguin Books.

Danner, Mark. 1997. America and the Bosnia genocide. *New York Review of Books* 44 (19): 55–65.

de Waal, Alex. 2005. *Famine that kills: Darfur, Sudan* (revised ed.). Oxford: Oxford University Press.

Garber, Steven. 2015. The common good. Guest sermon presented at St. Andrew United Methodist Church, Highlands Ranch, CO, August 23.

Glenny, Misha. 1999. *The Balkans: Nationalism, war, and the great powers, 1804–1999.* New York: Penguin Books.

Gutman, Roy. 1993. A daily ritual of sex abuse. *Newsday* (April 19): 1A.

Hill, Christopher R. 2014. *Outpost: Life on the frontlines of American diplomacy.* New York: Simon & Schuster.

Honig, Jan Willem and Norbert Both. 1996. *Srebrenica: Record of a war crime.* New York: Penguin Books.

Hukanović, Rezak. 1996. *The tenth circle of hell: A memoir of life in the death camps of Bosnia.* New York: Basic Books [orig. 1993].

Kristof, Nicolas. 2016. The killing field. *New York Times, Sunday Review,* February 27. Retrieved from http://www.nytimes.com/2016/02/28/opinion/sunday/the-killing-field.html

Mason, Gary. 2016. Reconcile: Steps toward peace and justice. Guest sermon delivered at St. Andrew United Methodist Church, Highlands Ranch, CO, February 28.

Ngor, Haing (with Roger Warner). 1987. *Haing Ngor: A Cambodian odyssey.* New York: Warner Books.

Power, Samantha. 2004. Dying in Darfur: Can the ethnic cleansing in Sudan be stopped? *The New Yorker* (August 30): 56–73.

Prunier, Gérard. 2005. *Darfur: The ambiguous genocide.* Ithaca, NY: Cornell University Press.

United States Holocaust Memorial Museum. 2000. Extermination camps. Unpublished manuscript, Wexner Learning Center, Washington, DC.

Van Arsdale, Peter W. 2008. Ethnicity as a basis of rebellion and division in Darfur. Africa Today Associates, paper presented at consultation on Darfur, Nairobi, Kenya, June 9–11.

Van Arsdale, Peter W. 2006. *Forced to flee: Human rights and human wrongs in refugee homelands.* Lanham, MD: Lexington Books.

Vulliamy, Ed. 2015. Bosnia's survivors gather and grieve as the soil endlessly gives up its dead. *The Guardian,* August 8. Retrieved from http://www.theguardian.com/world/2015/aug/08/bosnias-agony-continues-as-the-earth-endlessly-gives-up-its-dead-srebrenica

Welaratna, Usha. 1993. *Beyond the killing fields: Voices of nine Cambodian survivors in America.* Stanford, CA: Stanford University Press.

Chapter Five

Invisible Barriers
Children's Rights

AN IMAGE OF GOD

"For us, our daughter is like an image of god." Manish Kumar is speaking about his daughter, Kartika. He and his family live in India's Haryana state. His wife, Priya Kumar, says: "My husband was so delighted when our daughter was born. He distributed sweets to everyone in the neighborhood. There's really no difference [between having a boy and having a girl.]" In a region where boys often are favored over girls, where family economics often work against girls, and where feticide still is practiced, these statements are transformative from a human rights perspective, as Sonia Narang (2015) reports.

Feticide in India (i.e., the sex-selective abortion of female fetuses) is illegal. Yet it happens on a regular basis. It also is illegal for a doctor to reveal the sex of a fetus. Yet this also happens on a regular basis. Some doctors, induced by under-the-table payments, conduct ultrasounds and provide sonograms to prospective parents. These are then used to find out the sex of the fetus and, in turn, determine whether to keep or destroy it. Especially among many urban dwellers, where families are smaller, boys are favored over girls. As a boy grows up and seeks to marry, he usually remains with his family. His prospective bride must leave her family, bringing with her a dowry. This can amount to several thousand dollars' worth of gifts. This drains the wealth of her family, while bolstering the wealth of his. Some families therefore seek not to raise girls in this patriarchal, economically imbalanced environment. Over time, with feticide continuing in Haryana, this has led to a sex ratio that is the most disparate of any place in India: 879 women for every 1,000 men.

While some would argue that a fetus is not a child, others would disagree. Self-described human rights champions are forcing the issue, as Rhitu Chatterjee (2015) reports. Several have mounted sting operations against doctors that provide sonograms illegally; by entering the clinic as a "decoy" and obtaining the sonogram, then reporting the offense to local police, a pregnant "stinger" can contribute to the adjudication and imprisonment of such a doctor. At the national level, Prime Minister Narendra Modi is attacking the problem through a combination of law enforcement and public relations tactics. The practice of infanticide (i.e., the killing of a newborn, again usually a female) also is being targeted more aggressively than before. "We see it as genocide," says lawyer/activist Varsha Deshpande (quoted in Chatterjee 2015).

When the topic of children's rights is raised in Uganda, some citizens think not of infants but of older children. The "night commuters" discussed in the introduction often were able to escape the predations of the Lord's Resistance Army (LRA) in Uganda. Other children were not so lucky. A pastor working in northeast Democratic Republic of Congo, where the LRA fled in 2006, says that many children in his diocese have seen family members killed by the group's soldiers. "I've met more than a thousand children who have been abducted," he says (quoted in Christy 2015: 42).

When the topic of children's rights is raised in Ethiopia, some citizens think first of disabled children and their rights to an equal education. Some citizens of the United States think first of Native American, reservation-based children with special needs. Some citizens of Bangladesh think first of sweatshops, sexual abuse, and trafficking. These issues indeed are critical. When asked what should be done, these same citizens often state that "helping the victims" and "changing the system" are paramount. In fact, the situation is usually far more complicated. Invisible barriers must be identified and crossed.

In a speech to the Human Rights Council in Geneva on March 2, 2015, US Secretary of State John Kerry made the following statement:

> We've seen groups like Daesh [i.e., the Islamic State] burn human beings alive, barbarically behead prisoners, sell girls into slavery, and execute widely and indiscriminately. And recently, the UN reported the horrifying ways that Daesh treats even its most vulnerable captives: crucifying children, burying children alive, handpicking mentally challenged children to serve as suicide bombers and kill even more innocent people.

The abuse of children also includes the misuse of children, as commodities, to what Kerry termed "evil ends."

Some heroes and heroines go unrecognized. Yet their accomplishments, sometimes seemingly miraculous and under the harshest of conditions, can save lives and thus alter the course of history in a particular place, in a particular way. That is the case for Irena Sendler, whose story has been told by Marti Attoun (2003). She truly was "the woman who loved children."

Sendler saved nearly 2,500 children from death at the hands of the Nazis during World War II. Yet, as Attoun notes, her remarkable story was a footnote to history for almost 60 years. It was only when three Kansas schoolgirls, looking for a topic for a history contest, started exploring Sendler's life and the details emerged. In 1939 she was working for Warsaw's social welfare department. During 1940, after Germany had invaded Poland, she watched as nearly 350,000 Jews were packed into the tiny Warsaw Ghetto. A Catholic, she saw the increasing hardships they were facing. She guessed at what their ultimate fate might be. Joining Zegota, an underground network of activists, she soon was tasked with heading the operation to smuggle Jewish children out of the ghetto, to safety. With a forged permit, she went undercover as a nurse with the code name Jolanta. She creatively employed the three kinds of resources suggested as essential in chapter 1: human skills, networking, funding.

Aided by dozens of volunteers, "Jolanta" was able to smuggle children to private homes, orphanages, and convents in the Warsaw area. Some exited through sewer pipes, others in trunks, suitcases, and sacks carried surreptitiously by her colleagues. The youngest had to be sedated so potential crying would not be heard by Nazi guards. The rescue teams wrote down the names of every child possible, also noting their new Christian names—given so as to improve their survival chances once they were resettled. Yet, Sendler's efforts were discovered by the Gestapo in 1943, and she was imprisoned and beaten. Her survival was only assured when Zegota activists bribed a guard, allowing her to escape. Never touting or advertising what she had done, she died in 2008 in Warsaw at the age of 98.

CASE #1: CHILD ABUSE, NEGLECT, AND SEX TRAFFICKING IN THE UNITED STATES

It is difficult to estimate the number of children who are victimized by sex traffickers each year in the United States. The Polaris Project is among the most reputable organizations that track such statistics and—in conjunction with its National Human Trafficking Resource Center hotline—presented data indicating that 29.2 percent of the 5,544 trafficking cases, of all types, reported in 2015 involved

minors. A majority of these involved sex trafficking. Calls to the hotline from people in California were by far the most numerous of any
state (NHTRC 2015). In my hometown of Denver, Colorado, the underground sex trafficking economy (for victims of all ages) was estimated
at $39.9 million in 2007, the latest year for which data were available;
this large total, remarkably, was far less than estimates made for
seven other major US cities (Dank et al. 2014). And, these data do not
reveal the totality of people trafficked or money expended, since many
cases are not reported.

Correlates of sex trafficking, with a particular focus on the US,
include childhood abuse and neglect. As Jennifer Stith (2015) stresses,
not all abuse is sexual and not all trafficking of children is associated
with sexual abuse. Yet, it is substantial. The Wings Foundation, with
whom she works and which focuses on Colorado, estimates that one in
four girls and one in six boys nationwide experience some form of childhood sexual abuse before the age of 18. Few report it. As facilitated by
Stith, my colleagues and I heard the gripping firsthand account of a
woman named May. She told us how her grandfather had abused her
sexually from the age of three through the age of 15. She had repressed
the memories. She developed eating disorders and PTSD. Stith stated
that about 90 percent of those abused are victimized by someone they
know. To reduce the likelihood of being caught, such abusers will scare
their victims, as she illustrates: "If you tell anyone, they won't believe
you." "It was your fault." "This is our little secret." "I'll kill myself and
it will be on you." The Wings Foundation estimates that, just in Colorado, the long-term treatment, socioeconomic, and work productivity
costs of childhood sexual abuse is $21.5 billion.

Most of the children abused in this fashion are not trafficked.
But, they are at higher risk for trafficking. So are those who have been
neglected. Abuse is not the same as neglect, but the latter is more frequent in the US. As Gary Melton (2015, personal communication) has
noted, American service agencies, clinics, and law enforcement agencies receive about three million calls on this annually. The professions,
such as social work and law enforcement, hammer the "don't abuse"
ideology but don't hammer the "don't neglect" message. Victims of
both are at high risk for trafficking. Neglect is associated with poverty,
dysfunctional home environments, inadequate shelters for the homeless, inadequate health care, dysfunctional social service systems, and/
or drug abuse, in particular. Even the efforts of well-intended but
improperly prepared Good Samaritans can increase a child's risk
(Mitchell 2014). It should be added that, perhaps surprisingly, many of
those youngsters trafficked within the US are in the child welfare system. Their life experiences have increased their vulnerabilities.

A trafficker will approach and gain access to a child in any one of
several ways: entrapment, coercion, kidnapping, befriending. Some

traffickers meet their victims online, others in-person. Some use intermediaries to solicit contacts indirectly. Sometimes people well respected by the public, and "regularly in the public eye," are the perpetrators. Sometimes the children are paid, often they are not. From the perspective of parents, the situation can be terrifying. Not knowing what has happened, what the invisible barriers are, or understanding what kind of stranger has been involved instills worry and fear. Rumors can spread (Samuels 2015). It truly is, as Austin Choi-Fitzpatrick (2012: 24) emphasizes, part of a larger system of modern slavery and slaveholders perpetrating injustice.

Escape, exit, and rescue are the three most common ways children get out and get away. Yet none of these guarantee successful reintegration into one's community. Bold moves are being taken by officials and community residents in some jurisdictions. For example, in January 2015, in Jefferson County, Colorado, District Attorney Peter Weir created a first-of-its-kind unit for the state: It is aimed at helping at-risk children before they become victims of trafficking. Along with citizens, representatives of police departments and the county's human services department are key actors. According to Jesse Paul (2015: 1A), what sets this effort apart is "its progressive identification tool and 'team-based' approach of equal parts prevention and prosecution." A major analytic focus is on vulnerability and how it can be better understood from both county services' and perpetrators' angles. To paraphrase one representative, trafficking is not just "from elsewhere," it is "from here." Although outcomes associated with the effort cannot yet be evaluated, because it is so new, the intent—once at-risk children have been identified—is to establish "public safety nets."

Negative effects can last a lifetime. Unresolved child sexual abuse, including that associated with trafficking, can take many forms in adults. These include flashbacks, feelings of guilt or shame, addictions or compulsions, depression or suicidal thoughts, panic attacks, eating disorders or body image issues, problems with trust and intimate relationships, community or peer isolation, and decreased work productivity (Stith 2015).

Beginning with the George H. W. Bush administration, and continuing with the Barack Obama administration, US government efforts to battle human trafficking came more to focus on sex trafficking. Yet most of this focus has been on adult rather than child victims. Donald Bross (2015) is a leading legal expert regarding children. He serves as associate director for Pediatric Law, Policy, and Ethics at the Kempe Center for the Prevention and Treatment of Child Abuse and Neglect. When we met, he stressed that so much US law has been "aspiration-oriented"—about what's hoped for—as opposed to "legitimacy-oriented"—about what's really needed and will work. Meaningful child development depends on the latter. Both nationally and internationally, cross-referencing the UN Convention on the Rights of the Child is useful aspirationally but will make little difference if there are not local laws that are readily enforceable, together with targeted local resources. As Anne Gallagher (2012: 173) stresses, ultimately a human rights–based approach to trafficking, operationally directed, is needed.

CASE #2: THE CHIBOK GIRLS AND BOKO HARAM

On May 4, 2015, US Secretary of State John Kerry laid a commemorative wreath at a granite wall near the site of the devastating August 7, 1998, suicide bombing at the US Embassy in Nairobi, Kenya. He said, "Let us agree, the only place for al-Qaeda, al-Shabab, Boko Haram, Daesh [ISIS, Islamic State] and others like them is in the past. The future does not belong to them" (Kerry 2015). Within hours of this proclamation, and perhaps not coincidentally, the Nigerian government claimed that its soldiers had freed nearly 300 Boko Haram captives—many of them women and girls—during the preceding week. It was not initially clear as to whether any of those freed were among the so-called "Chibok girls," 276 of whom had been abducted from their school in April 2014. This incident made international headlines for months. Tragically, as the rescuing soldiers neared, it was reported that Boko Haram fighters stoned several girls to death (Faul 2015: 10A).

Boko Haram's origins can be traced to 2002. It sprang from an Islamic Salafist sect and initially claimed ties to al-Qaeda. Its founder, a fundamentalist preacher (later executed) named Mohammed Yusuf, "believed that the world was flat and the theory of evolution was a lie" (Hammer 2015: 61). From a northeast Nigerian base, since 2004 it has spread to Cameroon, Niger, and Chad. By mid-2015 it had proclaimed formal allegiance with ISIS and rebranded itself as the Islamic State's West Africa Province. By then it was estimated that several thousand people had been killed and more than a million displaced by its actions (ICG 2015). By early 2016 it was claimed that nearly two million had been displaced overall (Refugees International 2016). It also was estimated to have about 10,000 active fighters. Early that spring, some gains had been realized against Boko Haram in northeast Nigeria. The Sambisa Forest was a strategic area. Ironically, these strides in recapturing villages were being made by South African mercenaries, working at times side by side with but more often apart from Nigerian troops. The mercenaries were well equipped with armored personnel carriers, attack helicopters, night-vision goggles, and other weapons. They also were well trained. One unnamed official stated that the mercenaries were "in the vanguard in the liberation" but that their role was unofficial. Another said that they work mostly at night, then "the Nigerian Army rolls in [during the daytime] and claims success." "They're relics of apartheid," our colleague Jakkie Cilliers of the Institute for Security Studies in Pretoria, an affiliate of the Pardee Center at the University of Denver, was quoted as saying (Nossiter 2015). Such operations are officially barred by the South African government but, nonetheless, were unofficially proceeding full-force (Nossiter 2015).

As the International Crisis Group stresses, the Lake Chad Basin, spanning the borders of Nigeria, Chad, Cameroon, and Niger, is a center of jihadism. It is potentially resource rich, though underdeveloped, while also serving as a hub for the smuggling of people and illicit goods. Disaffected youth, corrupt political systems, and migration-driven tensions all serve to destabilize the region. One Western diplomat was quoted as saying that "predation is the generalized system of governance" (ICG 2015: 3). In northeast Nigeria, Boko Haram's home, political malfeasance and clientelism are rife. Impoverished people become disaffected people, and in the northeast the poverty rates are the highest of the country's six zones. Across the region, jobs are scarce.

Paradoxically, as the governments of Nigeria and Niger have increased their security budgets in an attempt to better fight Boko Haram, other sectors have suffered. Education and health are severely underfunded. Gender-based violence disproportionately impacts schoolgirls. Large numbers drop out long before completing middle or high school.

In addition to kidnappings and raids, both conventional and suicide attacks have been mounted by Boko Haram fighters. But this is not what wins over portions of the local populace. The sect claims to be "purifying the region from all the sins allegedly brought by democracy" (ICG 2015: 13). It denounces "Western" vaccination programs, including those involving polio. Its leader, Abubakar Shekau, is a powerful, enigmatic, and perhaps even part-fictionalized spokesman. The ominous mystique therefore is magnified. The development of parallel economic networks, unchecked by federal authorities, has allowed jobs to be created and charities to be formed by the sect. A quasi-administrative network even has emerged in some parts of northeast Nigeria.

Core–periphery relations are imbalanced in the Lake Chad Basin, and—as noted in chapter 4 in the discussion of Sudan—contribute systemically to the violence. With weak policing, the elite extract from those at the margins, criminal networks have space to expand, and traffickers move with impunity. The International Crisis Group notes that decades of state mismanagement have fostered alienation among traditionally conservative (often Christian) rural citizens. They have "easily been subdued by radical groups. Boko Haram, the most violent, has used weapons and intimidation to win local acquiescence but also [provided an alternative identity] that replaced the absent state" (ICG 2015: 8). Hans de Marie Heungoup (2015) states his findings bluntly: "[Most of its fighters] are forced recruits or people driven into the arms of Boko Haram by poverty."

Ambassador Amina Ali of the African Union made the following statement in a speech delivered at the University of Denver in March 2015:

> Boko Haram came about because of a lack of viable institutions. The African Union saw this, but can't simply rush in. When Chad decided to help, as a neighbor [of Nigeria], this was appropriate. U.S. assistance also is welcomed. It's radicalism, extremism, and terrorism. Boko Haram must be destroyed.

Nigeria must take the lead. The late Nigerian writer Chinua Achebe laid out a key, underlying problem years ago. He said it isn't just corruption, although this is pervasive. It isn't just subservience to foreign manipulations, although these have been severe. "It is the failure of our

AGENCY ACTION
The Human Trafficking Center

In 2002, the University of Denver's Josef Korbel School of International Studies initiated the Human Trafficking Clinic, now known as the Human Trafficking Center. Founded by Prof. Claude d'Estrée, it offers the only two-year, graduate level, professional training degree in human trafficking in the US. Recent guest speakers have included Kevin Bales, founder of *Free the Slaves*.

Issues involving children are regularly addressed. For example, research-based blogs are posted, covering topics such as child soldiers, child marriage, and the forced labor of children. A Human Trafficking Index is being developed. In its initial stages, it pulls information from the US Department of State's *Trafficking in Persons* report, including information on child soldiers, child marriage, the commercial sexual exploitation of minors (including sex tourism), and the forced labor of children in a variety of industries. The center also engages in research-based advocacy. It touts the kind of evidentiary-based empiricism stressed in chapter 1. Its representatives have testified on Colorado's SB 15-30, which provides for an affirmative defense to charges of prostitution if the person was a victim of sex trafficking, including minors. They also have testified on Colorado's HB 14-1273, the overhaul to the state's human trafficking law, which covers both the labor and sexual exploitation of minors (Hamaker 2016).

The center works in conjunction with the Colorado Human Trafficking Council, which is legislatively mandated. Master's degree graduates of this program have gone on to a variety of professional positions with NGOs, IGOs, educational institutions, and governmental agencies, both in the US and abroad.

rulers to reestablish vital links with the poor and dispossessed of this country" (1987: 141). Until Nigeria and neighbors like Chad are able to address long-standing grievances (such as those associated with girls' education), underdevelopment, and dispossession, it will be very difficult to drive out Boko Haram. Hundreds of militants have been arrested, especially in Niger, and hundreds of others have been killed, especially in Cameroon, but this has made little difference. Nigeria's oil wealth is not directed in ways that are helping. Nigerian military strategies derived from Western sources did little through the summer of 2015, but did gain momentum during the fall. A Nigerian Presidential Amnesty Program for ex-insurgents is in transition.

In the meantime, the families of the kidnapped "Chibok girls" continue to worry and wait. A strategy being employed by Margee Ensign, president of the American University of Nigeria, is helping. She has brought some of the girls who escaped the initial kidnapping to the university. There, on full scholarships, they are completing their secondary schooling before beginning college coursework. Ensign sees education as an enabling right, paralleling its reflection through the Tree of Rights and—beyond Boko Haram—hopes to combat corruption and governmental dysfunction with democracy, transparency, and tolerance (Hammer 2015). Perhaps even the anxieties associated with a March 2015 radio broadcast ultimately can be diminished. It was reported that some of the girls had been brainwashed into becoming suicide bombers, using explosives hidden under their *hijab* coverings. This was confirmed in grisly fashion in February 2016, when two kidnapped girls walked into the crowded Dikwa refugee camp in northeast Nigeria and detonated suicide vests; 58 people were killed (Umar 2016).

CASE #3: EUROPE'S MISSING REFUGEE CHILDREN

In January 2016, this startling headline appeared: "More than 10,000 unaccompanied child refugees have vanished following their arrival in Europe and may have fallen into the hands of organized trafficking gangs, EU's criminal intelligence agency says." The Europol chief of staff, Brian Donald, warned that a sophisticated pan-European "criminal infrastructure" had begun targeting European-bound refugees. He estimated that about 5,000 of the missing children had disappeared in Italy alone and that about 1,000 more were unaccounted for in Sweden. Europol estimated that, in total, as many as 270,000 children had come to Europe (including Scandinavia) in the recent waves from Syria and elsewhere (PressTV: 2016). Of this number, perhaps 10 percent arrived as unaccompanied minors (Townsend 2016).

From 2014 on, the backstory behind this crisis became increasingly well-known. Human rights advocates cringed as boat after boat crept across the Aegean Sea, at first bringing dozens, then hundreds, then thousands of desperate people fleeing Syria, Afghanistan, and Iraq. Further west, thousands crossed the Mediterranean Sea fleeing Eritrea, Nigeria, Somalia, and other African nations. Some used so-called "ghost ships," traveling at night. Greece usually was the immediate destination of the former, most transiting through Turkey. Italy usually was the immediate destination of the latter, most transiting through Libya. A majority of those arriving in Greece were women and children. Rubber rafts, flimsy wooden boats, and—occasionally—sleek ocean-worthy vessels were used. Some were run by reputable skippers, others by smugglers. Some refugees were forced to pay as much as US$5,000 per person. When nearly 1,200 people drowned—hundreds of them children—during April 2015, the phrase "European refugee crisis" entered common parlance, since virtually all those fleeing were seeking homes in Europe. Germany, Sweden, France, and Italy were receiving the largest numbers of asylum applications. During 2015, according to Eurostat (2016), 1,255,600 first-time seekers applied for asylum in the 28 European Union countries; 88,695 of these were unaccompanied minors. These totals represented over 70 percent increases compared with 2014.

The war in Syria has been particularly problematic. It began in 2011. Many analysts see it as the refugee crisis' central precipitant.

Two refugee girls sit with their father and grandmother in a European warehouse.

The concept of asymmetrical warfare was introduced in chapter 3, and the war in Syria represents asymmetry to the extreme. There are multiple, imbalanced, shifting factions. In one sense it is a civil war, with the regime of President Bashar al-Assad battling what it perceives to be rebels-*cum*-terrorists intent on destroying the national fabric. The rebels represent multiple factions, including most notably the Supreme Military Council of the Free Syrian Army, the Islamic Front, and Harakat Ahrar al-Sham al-Islamiyya, as well as extreme jihadist groups (e.g., ISIS) and Kurdish groups, namely the Popular Protection Units. In another sense it is a proxy war, with Russia and Iran supporting Assad's Alawite regime and the US (among other Western and Gulf Arab nations) supporting one or more rebel factions, most of whom are Sunni. In still another sense it is an international war, with ISIS having taken over large swaths of Syrian and Iraqi territory and being condemned by all the other parties, including Assad.

From the conflict's start in 2011 through early 2016, approximately 4.6 million Syrian refugees had fled to neighboring countries, with another 7.6 million estimated to be IDPs. As of February 2016 both Turkey (with over 2.5 million refugees from Syria) and Jordan (with over one million refugees from Syria) stated that they had reached the end of their "capacity to absorb" refugees (Guzel and Fraser 2016). During 2015, over one million refugees arrived in Europe, nearly half of these coming from Syria. The so-called London Conference, held in February 2016, brought the representatives of donor nations together. The United States continued as an especially generous non-European donor, pledging an additional $900 million toward the overall $9 billion effort. The European Commission estimated it would spend $9.2 billion in total on the refugee crisis during 2015–2016 as part of its evolving migration agenda (Duncan 2016).

The war is being fought on multiple fronts. There is no singular or simple divide. Children have been especially vulnerable as fronts have shifted village-to-village, camp-to-camp. In addition, it is estimated that several thousand may have been recruited as child soldiers, by all sides in the battle. Most of these fight as irregulars, or engage in spying, logistical assistance, and other "auxiliary" battle activities. Most are paid. Some are forced into criminal activity, which includes petty theft. Such conscripts are at risk for sexual and physical abuse. By early 2015 it was estimated that over 200 of these youngsters had been killed in the Syrian fighting (Mutter 2015).

Not all of those displaced in Syria are Syrians. Thousands are former Palestinian refugees, ironically displaced a second time owing to the current fighting. Many of their camps have been destroyed; others have been under siege for months (Gabiam 2015). The children among them have been put at "triple risk:" primary displacement (with aid dependency), secondary displacement (with greater aid dependency), cultural and psychosocial dissociation (internally and externally exacerbated). Some of these children are among those who later reached Europe, either unaccompanied or with family members.

Returning full circle to Europe's missing refugee children, it appears that many have been abducted by fast-growing criminal rings that did not exist until 2014. Others have been abducted by long-standing gangs that are "branching out and diversifying." Of the approximately 10,000 reported missing as of early 2016, all had registered with authorities (thus the number could be estimated). Many of these arrived unaccompanied. Mariyana Berket, of the Organization for Security and Cooperation in Europe (OSCE), stated: "Unaccompanied minors from regions of conflict are by far the most vulnerable population; those without parental care that have either been sent by their families to get into Europe first and then get the family over, or have fled with other family members" (quoted in Townsend 2016).

In October 2015, officials in Trelleborg, a town in Sweden, revealed that some 1,000 unaccompanied refugee children who recently arrived in this port town had gone missing. Several months later, in a separate report (again from Sweden), officials warned that many unaccompanied refugees had vanished and that there was "very little information about what happens after the disappearance" (quoted in Townsend 2016). The irony is that Sweden has been among the nations most open to assisting refugees during the past decade. It is possible that some of the children had been abducted by Swedish gangs as part of a recent anti-immigrant backlash. Xenophobia has been on the rise there.

There is no clear-cut correlation indicating that children at highest risk for abduction are those who were struggling to survive, for example in a Syrian refugee camp, before fleeing to Europe. But if inferences can be made from the work of ISPCAN, the International Society for the Prevention of Child Abuse and Neglect, it is possible that children who were at highest risk preflight would be those at highest risk for abduction postflight. Sex work and labor slavery are the likely reasons for most of the abductions, although it must be stressed that some of the missing could have been passed on to other family members in Europe "below the radar."

The criminals responsible for the missing refugee children are being pursued. Europol is at the forefront. Yet not enough is known about these criminal operations and infrastructure to do so systematically, country-by-country. "There are prisons in Germany and Hungary where the vast majority of people arrested and placed there are in relation to criminal activity surrounding the migrant crisis," said Brian Donald, Europol's chief of staff (quoted in Townsend 2016).

Ultimately, the symbolism can be stark. Two of the humanitarian-operated speed boats that pick up floundering refugees in the Aegean Sea are named in memory of two of the boys who drowned. Along with their family, they were attempting to make it to Europe.

WHAT'S BEING DONE

A Passionary

During the years immediately preceding World War II, an unassuming European found that compassion and risk taking go hand in hand—yet he never envisioned it that way. The late Nicholas Winton was not a hero, at least in his own book. He said he had never dodged a bullet, never been confronted by the secret police, never put his life on the line. Instead, he "wrote letters, made telephone calls, and composed lists. He liked lists" (A job well done 2015:82). He also believed in obligated action, and his methodically researched lists led directly to hundreds of children's lives being saved as World War II began.

On holiday in Prague in 1938, word got around that this English stockbroker might be able to help children—many orphaned or abandoned—escape to the West. They started coming to his door at the Europa Hotel with their stories, and he started making lists and taking photographs. From the British Home Office he obtained entry permits and located foster families for them. He organized rail transit to London. Once back in England, he continued this voluntary work. By late 1939, 669 children had been rescued from Czechoslovakia.

Having kept a scrapbook, but having sought no publicity for his efforts, he returned to his private life after the war. Nothing was heard about his accomplishment for half a century. However, when the scrapbook came to light in 1988, he became an instant sensation. Invited to appear on the *That's Life* TV show, he broke down when the studio audience greeted him; every one of them had been a child he had saved. Knighted by Queen Elizabeth, Sir Nicholas Winton died in 2015 at the age of 106. To the end, he said he "had simply done what needed doing at the time, in that place. Surely any decent person would have done the same?" (A job well done 2015:82). This is what obligated action means. This is what a passionary does.

An "Honor Killing" that Failed

A Girl in the River is the 2016 Academy Award-winning documentary about a Pakistani girl named Saba Qaiser. After falling in love and marrying, against her family's wishes, her father and uncle attempted to kill her, to "retain the family's honor." Despite being shot in the head and thrown into a river, she managed to crawl out. A rescuer called for help and Saba survived. When she had regained her strength, she began to speak out about this horrific abuse of rights. She began a determined encounter.

As reported by Nicholas Kristof (2016), Saba's story is amazing. He goes on to note that, on average, about one thousand "honor killings" take place in Pakistan annually. Citing this documentary, Pakistani Prime Minister Nawaz Sharif has promised to change the country's laws so as to crack down on such killings. Currently, blaming the victim and forgiving the killer—rather than systemic change and punishment—is the norm. The film's director, Sharmeen Obaid-Chinoy, hopes the documentary will start a viable national discourse on the issue. Kristof states: "[This type of injustice] is our century's great unfinished business."

Popular mobilizing around an outrageous practice like this might work. Legislated changes, tied to more enforceable laws, might work. Monitoring and advocacy by groups like Human Rights Watch might work. But, most importantly, that ever-necessary yet ever-amorphous force—political will—is essential.

Tackling Child Abuse and Neglect: Models that Work

The rights of children are among the most highly elaborated in the entire field of contemporary international law (Blitz 2011: 62). As noted in the concluding chapter, child maltreatment is being addressed aggressively cross-regionally and internationally. Much has been accomplished, many abuses have been averted, and many perpetrators have been brought to justice. The problem rests with gaps in actual protection, wherein some states do not recognize certain key covenants, do not enforce provisions they have ratified, or do not consistently follow up when pressed by human rights advocates. Since children's voices often go unnoticed, the gaps can be exacerbated.

As noted in chapter 3, "There's nothing so practical as a sensible theory." In the field of child abuse and neglect, several important theories and models have gained traction recently. One uses the acronym SEEK (Safe Environment for Every Kid). It is noted here because of its emphasis not on deficits (i.e., people's problems and gaps in service) but on strengths and resources (i.e., protective factors and viable interventions). Deficit models are being replaced by asset models. Innovative training protocols also are emerging (Dubowitz 2014). This movement indeed is leading to useful action.

The International Society for the Prevention of Child Abuse and Neglect (ISPCAN) is among the most innovative organizations dealing with child rights issues cross-culturally and transnationally. Models such as SEEK are incorporated into the research and training protocols ISPCAN promotes. Older research on "entry into" victimization is increasingly being augmented by newer research on "exit out of" victimization and into reintegration. ISPCAN's objectives include increasing awareness of child abuse problems; improving the quality of detection, treatment, and prevention efforts; disseminating academic and clinical research findings to relevant policy makers; and sharing "best practices" being developed by members and affiliates. Members range from mental health experts to law enforcement officials. They reside in over 100 countries (ISPCAN 2013).

Founded in 1977 on an all-volunteer basis, ISPCAN has evolved into an organization dependent upon both paid and nonpaid personnel. In my 2015 interview with its executive director, Steve Werner, the flexibility afforded by ISPCAN's organizational structure was stressed. Individuals, working groups, and affiliated organizations all have roles. In even-numbered years, major world congresses are hosted. In odd-numbered years, regional conferences are put on. Occasionally a "thinking space" is sponsored, so that creative ideas can rapidly be shared among members. The conference, training, and membership committees, representing the "organizational core," each are chaired by ISPCAN councilors, who are professionals from academia, child abuse centers, hospitals, and other related areas. Werner stressed that, rather than a board of directors, ISPCAN is governed by an elected board of knowledgeable councilors representing a diverse array of backgrounds.

Sex trafficking is of great concern to ISPCAN. While "reacting and rehabilitating" still remains the mantra of many erstwhile professionals dealing with such abuse, and while traditional processes of mandatory reporting and investigating appropriately continue, ISPCAN is increasingly promoting prevention and better understanding of revictimization. Understanding the "neighborhood context" therefore becomes critical; community influences are being analyzed more thoroughly. Where resources permit, safer environments are being created. More broadly, a "child rights framework" is being developed.

Among the countries that are moving more effectively to address child abuse and trafficking, India stands out. Its media, which has traditionally covered these issues as a form of "crime reporting," is improving, as is pragmatic conferencing among trained professionals (Taparia 2014). ISPCAN advocates are becoming much more vocal there.

> "[I advocate for the] girls who escaped Boko Haram in Nigeria and are still determined to learn, and girls in Pakistan and Kenya who have the chance to go to high school for the first time. My sisters inspire me to keep going. We know that we are part of something bigger."
> —Malala Yousafzai, the youngest-ever Nobel Prize winner, 2015

Achebe, Chinua. 1987. *Anthills of the savannah*. Oxford, UK: Heinemann.

Ali, Amina. 2015. The African Union: Current human rights and development issues. Speech by the A.U. Ambassador at Josef Korbel School of International Studies, University of Denver, Denver, CO, March 24.

Attoun, Marti. 2003. The woman who loved children. *Ladies' Home Journal* (December): 94–105.

Blitz, Brad. 2011. Neither seen nor heard: Compound deprivation among stateless children. In *Children without a state: A global human rights challenge*, ed. Jacqueline Bhabha, pp. 43–66. Cambridge, MA: MIT Press.

Bross, Donald. 2015. Personal communication from associate director, Kempe Center for the Prevention and Treatment of Child Abuse and Neglect, Aurora, CO, May 15.

Choi-Fitzpatrick, Austin. 2012. Rethinking trafficking: Contemporary slavery. In *From human trafficking to human rights: Reframing contemporary slavery*, ed. Alison Brysk and Austin Choi-Fitzpatrick, pp. 13–24. Philadelphia: University of Pennsylvania Press.

Chatterjee, Rhitu. 2015. How come there are no girls? Pregnant women in India want to know. *PRI's The World* (September 15). Retrieved from http://www.pri.org/stories/2015-09-14/how-pregnant-women-combat-sex-selective-abortion-india

Christy, Bryan. 2015. Tracking ivory. *National Geographic* 228(3): 30–59.

Dank, Meredith, Bilal Khan, P. Mitchell Downey, Cybele Kotonias, Debbie Mayer, Colleen Owens, Laura Pacifici, and Lilly Yu. 2014. Estimating the size and structure of the underground commercial sex economy in eight major US cities. *Urban Institute Research Report* (March 12). Retrieved from http://www.urban.org/research/publication/estimating-size-and-structure-underground-commercial-sex-economy-eight-major-us-cities

Dubowitz, Howard. 2014. The Safe Environment for Every Kid (SEEK) model: Helping promote children's health, development, and safety. *Child Abuse & Neglect* 38(11): 1725–1746.

Duncan, Pamela. 2016. Syria refugee crisis: Six charts that show how Europe is struggling to respond. *The Guardian,* February 3. Retrieved from http://www.theguardian.com/world/datablog/2016/feb/03/syria-refugee-crisis-and-international-aid-in-numbers

Eurostat. 2016. *Eurostat: The database of the European Union*. Directorate-General of the European Commission. Data accessible at: ec.europa.eu/eurostat.

Faul, Michelle. 2015. With rescue near, Boko Haram stoned Nigerian girls to death. *The Denver Post,* May 4, 10A.

Gabiam, Nell. 2015. The Syrian refugee crisis. Roundtable presentation, annual meeting of the American Anthropological Association, Nov. 18–22, Denver, CO.

Gallagher, Anne. 2012. Human rights and human trafficking: A reflection on the influence and evolution of the U.S. Trafficking in Persons reports. In *From human trafficking to human rights: Reframing contemporary slavery*, ed. Alison Brysk and Austin Choi-Fitzpatrick, pp. 172–194. Philadelphia: University of Pennsylvania Press.

Guzel, Mehmet and Suzan Fraser. 2016. Turkey hitting capacity. *The Denver Post,* February 8, 12A.

Hamaker, Rex. 2016. Personal communication from marketing and communications director, Human Trafficking Center, University of Denver, Denver, CO, January 9.

Hammer, Joshua. 2015. Escape from Boko Haram. *Smithsonian Magazine* 46(5): 56–67.

ICG. 2015. The Central Sahel: A perfect sandstorm. *International Crisis Group*, Africa Report No. 227 (25 June), Brussels.

ISPCAN (International Society for the Prevention of Child Abuse and Neglect). 2013. *Annual Report*. Aurora, CO: ISPCAN Secretariat.

A job well done. 2015. *The Economist* (July 11): 82.

Kerry, John. 2015. Remarks at wreath laying ceremony (May 4). *U.S. Department of State: Diplomacy in Action*. Retrieved from http://www.state.gov/secretary/remarks/2015/05/241426.htm

Kerry, John. 2015. Remarks at the 28th Session of the Human Rights Council, Geneva (March 2). *U.S. Department of State: Diplomacy in Action*. Retrieved from http://www.state.gov/secretary/remarks/2015/03/238065.htm

Kristof, Nicholas. 2016. Her father shot her in the head, as an "honor killing." *The New York Times,* January 31. Retrieved from mobile.nytimes.com/2016/01/31/opinion/sunday/her-father-shot-her-in-the-head-as-an-honor-killing.html

de Marie Heungoup, Hans. 2015. Cameroon's rising religious tensions. *International Crisis Group/African Arguments* (September 8). Retrieved from http://www.crisisgroup.org/en/regions/africa/central-africa/cameroon/op-eds/heungoup-cameroon-s-rising-religious-tensions.aspx

Melton, Gary B. 2015. Personal communication from co-editor of *Child Abuse & Neglect: The International Journal*, Aurora, CO, March 10.

Mitchell, Gregory. 2014. Book Review of *Life interrupted: Trafficking into forced labor in the United States*, by Denise Brennan. *Medical Anthropology Quarterly* 28(4): 22–24.

Mutter, Paul. 2015. Kids on the front lines. *U.S. News and World Report* (February 13). Retrieved from http://www.usnews.com/opinion/blogs/world-report/2015/02/13/the-rise-of-child-soldiers-in-syria

Narang, Sonia. 2015. It took a bride shortage for some northern India communities to realize the value of girls. *PRI's The World* (September 14). Retrieved from http://www.pri.org/stories/2015-09-14/it-took-bride-shortage-some-indias-northern-communities-realize-value-girls

NHTRC. 2015. Hotline statistics. *National Human Trafficking Resource Center*. Retrieved from http://traffickingresourcecenter.org/states

Nossiter, Adam. 2015. Mercenaries join fight against Boko Haram. *The New York Times,* March 13, A8.

Paul, Jesse. 2015. DA battling "unconscionable" trend. *The Denver Post,* February 27, 1A, 6A.

PressTV. 2016. 10,000 child refugees vanish after arrival in Europe: Europol (January 31). Retrieved from http://www.presstv.ir/Detail/2016/01/31/448043/Europe-European-Union-refugee-crisis-child-refugees-Europol-Brian-Donald-Italy-Sweden

Refugees International. 2016. The ones that got away. *Refugees International* (February 18). Retrieved from http://www.refugeesinternational.org/blog/2016/2/18/the-ones-that-got-away

Samuels, Annemarie. 2015. Narratives of uncertainty: The effective force of child-trafficking rumors in postdisaster Aceh, Indonesia. *American Anthropologist* 117(2): 229–241.

Taparia, Pooja. 2014. Between the lines: An analysis of media reportage on child sexual abuse. *ISPCAN: The Link* 23(2): 6–7.

Townsend, Mark. 2016. 10,000 refugee children are missing, says Europol. *The Guardian,* January 30. Retrieved from http://www.theguardian.com/world/2016/jan/30/fears-for-missing-child-refugees

Umar, Haruna. 2016. Girl tears off suicide vest, flees before Nigeria blast. *The Denver Post,* February 12, 20A.

Van Arsdale, Peter W. 2006. *Forced to flee: Human rights and human wrongs in refugee homelands.* Lanham, MD: Lexington Books.

Stith, Jennifer. 2015. Harnessing the power of the human spirit. Lecture sponsored by the Wings Foundation, delivered to the Rotary Club of Denver SE, Denver, CO, March 19.

Werner, Steve. 2015. Personal communication from executive director, International Society for the Prevention of Child Abuse and Neglect, Aurora, CO, March 10.

Yousafzai, Malala. 2015. Girls with goals. *The Economist/Special Edition: The World in 2016* (December): 92.

Chapter Six

Obligated Actions
Moral and Material Possibilities

AN OBLIGATION TO ACT

When our skills are sufficient, when our resources are available, and when we are confronted with assisting those under duress, whose rights have been abused, we must act. We have an obligation. "Obligation" does not mean "optional"; it means "duty" that leads to "tackling the opportunity." Practically speaking, while we cannot tackle every case relevant to our concerns (e.g., because of distance, timing, or funding), we can tackle every viable opportunity. When enacted, an obligation leaves a footprint. It represents a determined encounter.

Human rights and humanitarianism are linked. Humanitarianism is defined as "crossing a boundary" to assist; risk usually is encountered by the service provider or advocate as scarce resources are used to help the vulnerable, to help those whose rights have been abused. As we have noted elsewhere (Van Arsdale and Nockerts 2008), a theory of obligation emerges as the "morally possible" and the "materially possible" intersect. Notions of human dignity—reflecting the moral—are more appropriate as guides; notions of fairness and equity—reflecting the material—are more appropriate as humanitarian work is organized and implemented. "Burden sharing" is a process that reflects the moral, as decisions are made so that no one agency or person is overly taxed while helping; "use of appropriate service networks" is a process that reflects the material, as skilled providers and advocates are engaged. "Pragmatic humanitarianism" occurs as prin-

95

cipled guidelines and achievable actions merge, and as nonneutral stances are taken, as (for example) refugees are assisted. Humanitarian aid should be seen as representing a fundamentally moral/material relationship based on the obligation of "those who have, and can" to address the felt needs of "those who have not, and cannot" (Van Arsdale and Nockerts 2008). In the toughest of circumstances, we must be held accountable; our work must be "radical, revolutionary, and effective" (Waterston 2009: 13).

VIOLENCE: THE WORLDWIDE SITUATION

A centerpiece of this book has been the problem of structural violence. It has been shown to be insidious and widespread. More broadly, structural violence often is accompanied by other forms of violence, which includes spectacular violence as noted in chapter 3. In 2014 the World Health Organization released an important report on the status of violence, and violence prevention efforts, globally. (This report did not cover violence directly attributable to warfare and major internal conflicts.) Some remarkable findings can be shared. Less than half of countries reported mental health services to assist victims of violence. European and American countries offered the most and Africa the least. Globally, child protection services were the most widely reported of all countries (69%), followed by medico-legal services for victims of sexual violence. Adult protective services were the least common. Not surprisingly, the quality of all such services varied widely (WHO 2014: x).

The majority of countries (86%) reported laws providing victims with legal representation and participation in criminal courts, but far fewer (52%) reported having victim compensation legislation in place (WHO 2014: x). Increased efforts are underway, worldwide, to develop so-called "national action plans" to combat violence. Excluding warfare and major armed conflict, the types of violence being addressed overall are small-scale armed violence, gang violence, youth violence, child maltreatment, intimate partner violence, sexual violence, and elder abuse. Of 133 countries spanning six regions reporting progress with such plans, only in the Americas are more than 50 percent of countries engaged. Yet in the other five regions it is promising to note that none report less than 40 percent of countries engaged in such planning. Child maltreatment is the issue being addressed most aggressively cross-regionally. In contrast, gang violence plans are lagging cross-regionally. Several African nations are demonstrating leadership in addressing sexual violence. However, that violence prevention activities of all types often are not coordinated by a lead agency within a nation is disconcerting (WHO 2014: 24–26).

On March 9, 2015, Ramin Jahanbegloo asked this seemingly simple (but, in fact, extraordinarily complex) question at a forum sponsored by the University of Denver: As extreme jihadist violence is being considered, where is the "Muslim Gandhi," a person who is an extraordinary leader of peace-loving Muslims? As ISIS bulldozers began destroying Iraqi archaeological sites at about this same time, a UNESCO heritage specialist labeled the destruction a war crime; still another specialist labeled this violence a form of "cultural cleansing" (Yacoub and Salama 2015: 15A). Who, they asked, can stop it? Who, others asked, can comprehend it?

CHAMPIONS AND PASSIONARIES

Who, indeed? Obligated actions require committed individuals. Champions and passionaries come in all shapes, sizes, and styles. Some rely on oral prowess (like Carter Ham, chapter 3), others on written acumen (like Helen Abyei, chapter 4), others on gritty on-site action (like Jockin Arputham, chapter 2). While most are well educated, some are not. While most are able-bodied, some are not. While

PASSIONARY　　Amy Lynn Niebling

Amy Niebling passed away on February 3, 2005, in a plane crash in Afghanistan. She had been on assignment, doing what she loved—helping establish women's community health programs. Margaret Thompson and I were among her professors at the University of Denver, where she earned her master's degree in International and Intercultural Communication. As Thompson (2005: 6) later wrote in remembrance, before Amy graduated, "I encouraged Amy to be patient, confident that sooner or later she would find her one true passion, combining her interests in communication, media, culture, and international affairs." I, in turn, had talked to Amy about the value of overseas work, where she could serve as a humanitarian, given her passion for human rights. She had high standards, was very interested in ethics, and wanted to serve less fortunate people in practical ways.

Shortly after graduation Amy landed her "dream job," as a communications associate for Management Sciences for Health (MSH), a global NGO based in Boston. As Thompson also wrote, Amy's tasks "included developing and steering MSH's overall communications efforts, and developing media contacts to increase awareness of MSH's global activities." As she then came to assist at-risk Afghan women, she was "following her dream [and] in that way, Amy did make a difference in this world."

some are towering physically, others are diminutive. A few are famous, most are not. What all have in common is the ability to recognize severe abuse, distress, dislocation, disenfranchisement, or other inhumane situations, and to act humanely. Some act by serving, others through the creation of policy, others through applied research, still others by teaching. Champions and passionaries understand suffering but do not dwell on it. They understand that "compassion" is more than a philosophical term.

Compassion and Risk Taking

With obligated actions, compassion and risk taking often go hand in hand. As William Doino Jr. (2013) reports, so do surprising twists as a champion emerges. From 1943 through early 1945, Monsignor Hugh O'Flaherty of the Vatican, aided by Italians, helped hide nearly 4,000 American and British servicemen from Nazi and Gestapo pursuers. He also assisted many Jews. He earlier had toured POW camps and come to appreciate the miseries inflicted therein. Suspecting that O'Flaherty was assisting the Allies, the Nazi's Lt. Col. Herbert Kappler tracked him relentlessly but failed to capture him. O'Flaherty's daring earned him the nickname, "Scarlet Pimpernel of the Vatican." Eventually—as World War II ended—it was Kappler who was captured, then tried and imprisoned. His only regular visitor while in prison was O'Flaherty. In 1959, Kappler converted to Catholicism. O'Flaherty died in 1963 but has never been forgotten, particularly by his Irish brethren, who—along with others from all over the globe—honored him in a commemorative ceremony in Killarney in October 2013.

Sometimes the human rights champion comes as a surprise. Garry Kasparov of Russia, with a reported IQ of 190, is a former World Chess champion and current political activist. He sits on the board of the Human Rights Foundation. He helped found the Committee of 2008, a group of Russian freedom advocates. This activity is risky. His writings are widely acclaimed and have appeared in such publications as *The Wall Street Journal, The New York Times,* and *The Daily Beast.*

Taking large risks is current human rights champion and passionary George Tuto. Himself a migrant from Sudan, he now lives in Colorado but regularly travels to the Nuba Mountains, bordering Sudan and South Sudan. Often working with the Nuba Christian Family Mission, a faith-based organization, he brings food and medicine surreptitiously to Nuba people who have been targeted by Omar al-Bashir and his government with ferocity since 2012. Many have been forced to live in caves. On the ground, Tuto must be wary as he evades Sudanese troops and fighter aircraft. Barrel bombs, cluster bombs, and land mines are constant threats. His voluntary work is faith based. His colleague, Pastor Heidi McGinness, describes him as "a man of obligated action." In August of 2015, Tuto told several of us: "It's not easy to go [to help], but you can see a door opening. These are my people."

Institutional Innovations and Political Diplomacy

Obligated actions are increasingly taking new institutional forms. The Bill & Melinda Gates Foundation is not just awarding grants, it is directly investing in certain initiatives. For example, as the West African Ebola crisis of 2014–2015 continued, the foundation learned about CureVac, a biopharmaceutical company developing a potential "fast-track vaccine." "It not only took note—it took a stake in the company," reported Sarah Max (2015: B1). The $52 million in equity put forward allowed the foundation to embark on what is termed early-stage investing, a strategy that gives it a say in which avenues should be emphasized. In addition to health care, program-related investments are being made by the Gates Foundation in education, agriculture, and financial services for the poor.

Obligated actions can be reflected in the work of diplomats. Political diplomacy was used in a recent case involving genocide. In a remarkable circumstance, former Guatemalan dictator Efraín Ríos Montt stood trial and was convicted on charges of genocide in May 2013. As Peter Benson (2014) emphasizes, this is of great importance when viewed through both a human rights and a historical lens. This was the first time that a former head of state was tried and convicted of genocide crimes by his own nation's judicial system. Diplomats helped pave the way. (After appeal and review, a first retrial began in 2015 and a second in 2016.) Decades earlier, thousands of predominantly Maya Guatemalan villagers had been killed or maimed or had disappeared in wave after wave of governmentally sponsored persecution and violence. The Guatemala Scholars Network, comprised of several hundred scholars and other professionals, persevered for years, aiding the human rights cause by affording venues for diverse voices, by advocating for political change, and by sharing information throughout Europe and North America (in addition to Central America). The Guatemalan Forensic Anthropology Foundation, having worked to reconstruct much of the history surrounding the massacres, provided key evidence used by the tribunal.

I have discussed obligated actions and political diplomacy with Emmanuel Weyi. As a recent candidate for the presidency of the Democratic Republic of Congo (DRC), and as a successful businessman with no previous political experience, he believes he can offer fresh insights and definitive leadership. He told me that attention to human rights should be coparamount for DRC, along with attention to natural resource development, business development, and educational

development. Improved employment opportunities for younger Congo-
lese will emerge as correlates. Given the often-tragic history that the
human rights regime has experienced in his homeland, he is cautiously optimistic that changes can be implemented. He believes a new
treaty among Rwanda, Uganda, Tanzania, Burundi, and DRC—where
"everybody is watching everybody's back"—would help (Zavis 2016).
He is cognizant of what Carolyn Nordstrom (2009), as noted in chapter
3, calls "fracture zones." Weyi traces his emergent political interest to
the grounding he received from his father and mother; one offered useful advice, the other offered useful discipline. That he is a recognized
tribal chief is a plus, because his philosophy of action has roots in traditions of tribal justice.

Sometimes institutional innovations are for naught. Political
diplomacy and resulting political actions can become twisted and perverse. According to Amnesty International, about 120 lawyers and
support staff were rounded up across China during July 2015. Most
were human rights and civil rights specialists. Most had been working
on the cases of ordinary citizens who had complaints against the state.
The Beijing-based law firm Fengrui became a particular focus. Its lawyers regularly represent dissidents and also sue on behalf of people

Information about human rights and related issues can best be obtained firsthand, through on-site interviews. Here the author discusses recent events
with a man in the Southeast Asian nation of Timor-Leste.

forcibly evicted from their homes. To senior Chinese leaders, it appears that "obligated action" and "rule of law" mean suppressing discontent and suppressing the efforts of innovative legal activists. Even feminists have been held for campaigning against sexual harassment on public transport (Uncivil 2015).

My colleague Derrin Smith and I (Van Arsdale and Smith 2010) believe "expeditionary diplomacy" has merit. Marrying principles of institutional innovation, such as quick-and-ready multidisciplinary field response teams, with key diplomatic practices, such as skilled oration and mediation, "expeditionary forces" of a new sort could be dispatched to areas of conflict. They would not spend most of their time in offices or writing reports. Most of their time would be spent engaging diverse parties and adversaries in the field. Enhanced by ethnographic expertise, NGOs and IGOs would feed them their best ideas, using applied social scientists as liaisons.

THE NEXT FRONTIER: GAY RIGHTS

The Tree of Rights grows and expands in intriguing ways. Gay rights may best represent the next frontier in the quest for improved global human rights. As activists confront discrimination and societal fractures, the problems of structural violence become apparent. Nowhere are the challenges greater than in Africa.

Anti-Gay Legislation and Persecution in Africa

The fight for human rights always has political, economic, and cultural ramifications. It often has legislative ramifications as well; policies are crafted as lives are on the line. This is the case as gay rights are being pursued in Uganda against heavy odds. After years of acrimonious debate, the Uganda Anti-Homosexuality Act of 2014 was signed into law in February of that year by President Yoweri Museveni. Although it was soon overturned by the nation's high court on technical grounds, as DaMon Mosley (2015) reports, a new version of the law still is being pursued. Gay activities—and therefore gay rights—are not seen as "culture friendly," as "normal," or as "politically correct."

As originally drafted, the bill's purpose was to protect the "traditional [Ugandan] family by prohibiting . . . any form of sexual relations between persons of the same sex" while also prohibiting "the promotion or recognition of such sexual relations in public institutions and other places through or with the support of any Government entity in Uganda or any non-governmental organization inside or outside the country" (Government of Uganda 2009). At the extreme, the penalty of death was being considered for violators. Imprisonment was viewed as essential punishment.

Perceived Western imperialism is one reason that Uganda has taken this stance. The country claims it does not want to be beholden to "progressive, imposed interests." With the United States rapidly accepting pro-gay stances, from employment to marriage equality, such interests are seen as antithetical to Ugandan norms and to what was referred to in the original legislation as its "cherished culture." Yet, in one significant way, this stance is paradoxical, because key Western interests indeed are operative. Pro-gay research advocates, working internationally, have traced central elements of Uganda's anti-gay sentiment to the radical writings and speeches of American pastor Scott Lively. According to Mariah Blake (2014), he first visited the country in 2002. He began cultivating ties with influential politicians and religious leaders who themselves were anti-gay. In Kampala, the capital, Lively gave speeches to parliamentarians and cabinet members, containing themes that were later reproduced by them. One major theme: Western pro-gay agitators are trying to spread "the disease" of homosexuality, a disease that will "infect" Uganda's children. "They're looking for other people to be able to prey upon," he proclaimed. American evangelicals who visited in 2009 built upon this theme. As Mosley (2015) stresses, this type of rhetoric demonizes gay community members who already are vulnerable. (A Ugandan paper, *Rolling Stone,* earlier had published the names of the country's "100 top gays and lesbians," including their photos, addresses, and other contact information. One headline said: "Hang them.")

Similar themes have played out in Cameroon. Homosexuality (or its practice) is illegal there, as well as in 37 other African countries. As Pyper Scharer (2014) points out, same-sex activity in Cameroon is punishable by severe fines and imprisonment of up to five years. According to Article 347 of the penal code, with previsions dating from 1972, such penalties are faced by "anyone who performs homosexual acts whether in public or private, or who commits or is a party to the commission of any act of gross indecency with another person from the same sex" (Ndjio 2012, as reported in Scharer 2014: 25). While the law *de jure* only is intended to punish homosexual conduct, it *de facto* is used to persecute homosexual individuals. According to Cameroonian anthropologist Basile Ndjio:

> [State representatives] take advantage of the vague and imprecise character of this law, which allows for the arbitrary and fanciful interpretation of gays' and lesbians' sexual behavior as an "affront to public decency" and "contrary to accepted standards of sexual behavior." . . . [The idealized male, the Muntu] has been trained, instructed, required or urged to be disgusted by other forms of sex-

ual desire [as a threat] to both his manliness and his Africanness.
(quoted in Scharer 2015: 26)

That the Muntu may take abusive advantage of women without penalty is ironically beside the point.

Boko Haram's foothold in Cameroon further exacerbates the problem. Complex religious forces are at play. Traditional Sufi Islam is being challenged by fundamentalist Islamist ideology linked to Salafism. As Hans de Marie Heungoup (2015) stresses, historical Protestant and Catholic churches are facing competition from Islamic conversions and from Christian revivalist churches. What he terms "the seeds of intolerance" are increasingly being planted. While Cameroon does not have a history of religious violence, such intolerance may change that fact.

Gay persons harassed and persecuted in Cameroon face arbitrary detention, imprisonment, physical abuse, emotional abuse, and alienation. Fear-based tactics serve a repressive function. As in Uganda, the generalized "victim" of homosexuality in Cameroon is alleged by state officials to be the culture or the society itself.

The situation in The Gambia also has been dire. On February 18, 2014, President Yahya Jammeh (who seized power in a coup in 1996) reportedly said: "We will fight these vermins, called homosexuals or gays, the same way we are fighting malaria-causing mosquitoes, if not more aggressively" (HRC 2015: 27). Several months later, police in The Gambia conducted raids that led to the arrest of 12 men "on suspicion" of being gay. This coincided with the National Assembly's passage (and Jammeh's subsequent signing) of a bill allowing lifetime imprisonment for "aggravated homosexuality." Same-sex activity had been criminalized years earlier.

The Deaths of African Activists

Uganda's most well-known gay rights activist, David Kato, was beaten to death with a hammer on January 26, 2011. This was shortly after winning a lawsuit against a magazine that had called for his execution. In Cameroon, the body of leading gay rights activist Eric Ohena Lembembe was found in his home in the capital, Yaoundé, on July 15, 2013. He had been burned over much of his body with an iron. As Scharer (2014) reports, in the weeks prior to his murder he had issued a public denunciation of break-ins and other kinds of mayhem that had targeted gay rights advocacy groups.

One of South Africa's most famous lesbian rights activists was Noxolo Nogwaza. She was raped, then stoned and stabbed to death, on April 24, 2011. She was a member of the Ekurhuleni Pride Organising Committee. It was claimed that her abuse was a form of "corrective rape," perpetrated by men who are attempting to "convert" their victims to heterosexuality. Human Rights Watch labeled the death a hate crime (South African killing 2011). This attack was doubly concerning given the seemingly tolerant and progressive atmosphere that had come to prevail in South Africa. In 1996 the new constitution explicitly banned discrimination based on sexual orientation. This was one of a number of postapartheid human rights advances: Same-sex sexual activity is legal; same-sex marriage is legal; discrimination in employment is illegal; and ability to openly serve in the military is legal. Gay pride parades are held regularly in some of the larger cities. A number of gay rights advocacy groups are active. While harassment of gay persons has diminished, the general situation might be described as uneven. Certain of the country's liberal laws do not reflect the beliefs of a large swath of conservatives. Public polling indicates strong anti-gay sentiments. In 2014 several key South African leaders called for the repeal of the constitution's antidiscrimination provision.

WHAT'S BEING DONE

The UN Human Rights Committee has specified that the criminalization of homosexuality is incompatible with Article 17 and Article 19 of the long-standing International Covenant on Civil and Political Rights. Issues of privacy and freedom of opinion are at play. Building on this, information leaders and activists working in countries such as Uganda, Cameroon, and The Gambia are suggesting a combination of international pressure and local grassroots activism. International sanctions can make a difference. Applied field researchers, gathering carefully documented data, also can make a difference. The International Gay and Human Rights Commission, given its broad international support, provides a widely respected voice. That it holds consultative status (as a recognized NGO) at the United Nations is a plus.

The US-based Human Rights Campaign (HRC) has been aggressive in its response to anti-gay attitudes and activities in the United States and abroad. In response to what has been occurring in The Gambia, in November 2014 HRC formally condemned the legislation referenced earlier and then in December met with Gambian human rights activists. A strategy to impose a visa ban on President Jammeh and his colleagues, along with freezing his US assets, was proposed. President Barack Obama was presented with a petition urging strong action. Soon thereafter, another petition containing nearly 18,000 signatures was delivered to US Secretary of State John Kerry. Six days later, The Gambia was dropped from a preferential trade agreement, the African Growth and Opportunity Act. The pressure continues, led by HRC Global (HRC 2015: 27).

From a US perspective, the situation in Uganda is more complicated. The primary aid arm of the US government, USAID, has a major presence there. It employs nearly 16,000 people, making it one of the country's single largest employers. With an active annual portfolio approaching \$1.5 billion, Uganda is one of Africa's largest American aid recipients. Health, education, and governance are among the sectors being targeted. As noted by USAID's Philip Greene (2015, personal communication), leverage can be exerted in intriguing ways when human rights are being abused. Rather than "integrating" with Uganda's current development strategy, the United States—following the lead of its Department of State—is only "complementing" it. The gay rights situation is well understood and is a primary reason for this strategy. This means that USAID is exerting indirect pressure; it is an arm of the Department of State. The US does not tell other countries—outright—to accept gay persons, but at times it does maneuver in creative and helpful prorights, proacceptance fashion. That other innovative human rights initiatives are underway in Uganda, such as the Chain of Hope Rehabilitation Center (educating victims of child trafficking), will only help the gay rights campaign.

In a country such as South Africa, where pro-gay statutes are often not matched by on-the-ground attitudes and actions, international pressure and grassroots activism also are important. So are the voices of celebrities. There, the 2013 visit of the then-first lady of France, Valerie Trierweiler (who has supported same-sex marriage in her homeland), brought attention to lesbian issues through the interviews and affirming press conferences she held (Agence France Presse 2013). The outspoken persistence of local organizations such as South Africa's Forum for the Empowerment of Women is meaningful. The clout afforded by the US-based Human Rights Campaign can prove substantial, since it also works transnationally. The on-site investigations of reputable advocacy organizations such as Human Rights Watch and Freedom House also are influential; their published reports are widely read.

Also widely read are the works of Nigerian-born novelist Chinelo Okparanta. Her latest book is entitled *Under the Udala Trees* (2015). Featuring war, inequality, family, and a love forbidden by society, she provides a critical account of the struggle of the LGBTQ community in the Nigeria of the 1960s and 1970s. The constructs of womanhood, patriarchy, sexuality, and violence all are boldly developed in what Okparanta calls "a political call to action."

The most important celebrity in this arena is South African Archbishop Desmond Tutu, a Nobel Prize laureate. He is openly pro-gay. As I listened to him speak at a rally in Denver, Colorado, a decade ago, I was impressed with his ability to blend passion with intelligence, and to deliver a human rights message that was extremely compelling. Tolerance of diversity combined with peaceful activism was the central theme. Three thousand people stood and roared their approval.

> *"If a person is gay and seeks God and has good will, who am I to judge?"*
>
> —Pope Francis, 2015 (quoted in Goldberg)

JUST DO IT!

Nike proclaims "Just do it!" By building upon the Tree of Rights, which serves as a dynamic metaphor, as well as on the theory of structural violence, which indicates the insidious nature of rights abuses, straightforward interventions can be undertaken. Rather than mere reliance upon published guidelines, I have emphasized how important it is to use cases—past and present—that span cultural boundaries. I also have emphasized the roles played by champions and passionaries, who take their obligated actions seriously.

Champions continue to energize the gay rights campaign. The Stonewall Inn in New York City is considered by many to be the birthplace of the modern gay liberation movement in the United States. In 1969 it was the site of the so-called Stonewall Riots, thought to be the movement's single most important galvanizing event in the US. The 1995 movie *Stonewall* and the 2007 stage play of the same name added to the legacy. In 2015 the inn received official landmark status from the New York City Landmarks Preservation Commission for its historic catalytic role. Frank Kameny emerged, post-Stonewall, as a founder of the Gay Liberation Movement. A champion and passionary, he did it.

> *"It is a beautiful thing to be on fire for justice."*
>
> —Cornell West, 2015

Agence France Presse. 2013. Valerie Trierweiler, French first lady, meets gay rights advocates in South Africa. *Huff Post Queer Voices* (October 14). Retrieved from www.huffingtonpost.com/2013/10/15/valerie-trierweiler-gay-rights-groups-_n_4098735.html

Benson, Peter. 2014. Year in review, public anthropology, 2013: Webs of meaning, critical interventions. *American Anthropologist* 116(2): 379–389.

Blake, Mariah. 2014. Meet the American pastor behind Uganda's anti-gay crackdown. *Mother Jones* (March 10). Retrieved from www.motherjones.com/politics/2014/03/scott-lively-anti-gay-law-uganda

Doino, William, Jr. 2013. Hugh O'Flaherty, Ireland's shining priest. *First Things: Journal of Religion and Public Life.* Retrieved from http://www.firstthings.com/web-exclusives/2013/11/hugh-oflaherty-irelands-shining-priest

Goldberg, Susan. 2015. From the editor: Getting close to the Pope. *National Geographic* 228(2, August): ii.

Government of Uganda. 2009. The anti-homosexuality bill. Bills Supplement No. 13, Bill No. 18, to Uganda Gazette. Retrieved from www.publiceye.org/publications/globalizing-the-culture-wars/pdf/uganda-bill-september-09.pdf

Greene, Phillip. 2015. Personal communication from East African economic representative, United States Agency for International Development, Denver, CO, April 15.

HRC. 2015. Putting the pressure on The Gambia. *Equality: Human Rights Campaign* (Late Winter/Early Spring): 27.

de Marie Heungoup, Hans. 2015. Cameroon's rising religious tensions. *International Crisis Group / African Arguments* (September 8). Retrieved from http://www.crisisgroup.org/en/regions/africa/central-africa/cameroon/op-eds/heungoup-cameroon-s-rising-religious-tensions.aspx

Max, Sarah. 2015. From the Gates Foundation, direct investment, not just grants. *The New York Times,* March 13, B1, B7.

Mosley, DaMon. 2015. A regression in human rights: Uganda's anti-homosexuality bill is a major setback for East Africa. Unpublished manuscript, Josef Korbel School of International Studies, University of Denver, Denver, CO.

Nordstrom, Carolyn. 2009. Global fractures. In *An anthropology of war: Views from the frontline*, ed. Alisse Waterston, pp. 71–86. New York: Berghahn Books.

Okparanta, Chinelo. 2015. *Under the udala trees.* New York: Houghton Mifflin/Harcourt.

Scharer, Pyper. 2014. Out in the bush: Persecution and prosecution of gays and lesbians in Cameroon. *The Applied Anthropologist* 34(1/2): 25–28.

South African killing of lesbian Nogwaza 'a hate crime.' 2011. *BBC News* (May 3). Retrieved from www.bbc.com/news/world-africa-13265300

Thompson, Margaret. 2005. Remembering Amy Niebling. *GSIS News* 3(2, Summer): 6.

Uncivil: China says that by locking up lawyers it is defending the rule of law. 2015. *The Economist* (July 18). Retrieved from http://www.economist.com/news/china/21657828-china-says-locking-up-lawyers-it-defending-rule-law-uncivil

Van Arsdale, Peter W. and Regina A. Nockerts. 2008. A theory of obligation. *Journal of Humanitarian Assistance* (May 12). Retrieved from https://sites.tufts.edu/jha/?s=van+Arsdale

Van Arsdale, Peter W. and Derrin R. Smith. 2010. *Humanitarians in hostile territory: Expeditionary diplomacy and aid outside the Green Zone.* Walnut Creek, CA: Left Coast Press.

Waterston, Alisse. 2009. Introduction: On war and accountability. In *An anthropology of war: Views from the frontline*, ed. Alisse Waterston, pp. 12–31. New York: Berghahn Books.

West, Cornell. 2015. "Firebrand." *Smithsonian* 45(10): 64–65.

WHO. 2014. *Global status report on violence prevention*. Geneva: World Health Organization.

Yacoub, Sameer N. and Vivian Salama. 2015. Terrorists rip up ruins. *The Denver Post,* March 8, 15A.

Zavis, Alexandra. 2016. Meet the Colorado businessman who is running for president in Congo. *Los Angeles Times,* March 16. Retrieved from http://www.latimes.com/world/africa/la-fg-congo-candidate-20160316-story.html

Glossary of Acronyms

AAA	American Anthropological Association
AFRICOM	US African Command
AIDS	acquired immune deficiency syndrome
ANC	African National Congress
AU	African Union
APB	Atrocities Prevention Board
CBO	community-based organization
CMMB	Catholic Medical Mission Board
CRRIC	Collaborative Refugee and Rights Information Center
DRC	Democratic Republic of Congo
FBI	Federal Bureau of Investigation
GDP	gross domestic product
HRC	Human Rights Campaign
HRSP	Human Rights and Special Prosecutions
HSI	Homeland Security Investigations
ICG	International Crisis Group
IDP	internally displaced person
IED	improvised explosive device
ICC	International Criminal Court
ICG	International Crisis Group
ICU	Islamic Court Union
IGO	intergovernmental organization
ISIS	Islamic State of Iraq and the Levant
ISPCAN	International Society for the Prevention of Child Abuse and Neglect
IUU	illegal, unreported, unregulated
JEM	Justice and Equality Movement
LGBTQ	lesbian, gay, bisexual, transgender, queer

LLC	limited liability company
LRA	Lord's Resistance Army
MSF	Médecins Sans Frontières (Doctors Without Borders)
MSH	Management Sciences for Health
NGO	nongovernmental organization
NHTRC	National Human Trafficking Resource Center
NPR	National Public Radio
OM&R	operation, maintenance, and repair
OPM	Organisasi Papua Merdeka (Papuan Freedom Organization)
OSCE	Organization for Security and Cooperation in Europe
OSS	Office of Strategic Services
PBS	Public Broadcasting System
PNG	Papua New Guinea
POW	prisoner of war
PTSD	posttraumatic stress disorder
SEEK	Save Environment for Every Kid
SLA	Sudanese Liberation Army
SPLM	Sudan People's Liberation Movement
SS	Schutzstaffel (Protective Squadron)
SSICC	Somali Supreme Islamic Courts Council
TEDMED	licensed annual conference on health and medicine
UN	United Nations
UNESCO	United Nations Educational, Scientific and Cultural Organization
UNHCR	United Nations High Commissioner for Refugees
UNICEF	United Nations Children's Fund
USAID	United States Agency for International Development
USDA	United States Department of Agriculture
USSR	Union of Soviet Socialist Republics
WASH	water, sanitation, hygiene
WFP	World Food Programme
WHO	World Health Organization

Index

Abyei, H., 5, 61, 97
Achebe, C., 84
Afghanistan, 86, 97
Africa
    anti-gay legislation and persecution
        in, 101–103
    deaths of gay rights activists in,
        103–104
    postapartheid human rights advances
        in, 104
    See also Burundi, Cameroon, Chad,
        Democratic Republic of Congo, Dji-
        bouti, Eritrea, Ethiopia, Gambia
        (The), Kenya, Libya, Rwanda,
        Niger, Nigeria, Somalia, South
        Africa, South Sudan, Sudan, Tan-
        zania, Uganda
African Charter for Human and People's
    Rights, 2
African Union, 31, 84
AFRICOM, 40, 61
Ahmed, S. S., 29
Alam, 46–47
al-Assad, B., 87
al-Bashir, O., 65, 67, 75, 98
Alemu Worku, K., 49, 53–54
Alexander, K. L., 2
Ali, A., 84
al-Mahdi, S., 75
al-Qaeda, 31, 82
al-Shabaab, 29–31, 82
American Anthropological Association,
    Declaration on Human Rights, 5
Amum, P., 35, 61
Angka. *See* Khmer Rouge

Ap, A. 47
Applebaum, A., 43
Archaeological heritage sites, purposeful
    destruction of, 18
Arendt, H., 12
Arputham, J., 26, 97
Asher, M., 34
Asymmetrical warfare, 30, 40–41, 47, 55,
    87
Atrocities Prevention Board, HRSP, 49
Attoun, M., 79
Auma-*cum*-Lakwena, A., 3
Australia, 52
Autonomy, sphere of, 10
Awom, Melkianus (General), 47

Barre, Zaid (General), 28
Behavioral change, punishment as inef-
    fective driver of, 54
Benevolence, 9
Benson, P., 99
Berket, M., 88
Bill & Melinda Gates Foundation, 99
Blake, M., 102
Blitz, B., 90
Boko Haram, 82–85, 103
Bosnia's Omarska concentration camp,
    69–74
Both, N., 70
Botta, R., 22, 24, 26
Bross, D., 81
Brown, J., 19
Bulcha, M., 42–45
Burundi, human rights violations in, 2, 100
Bush, G. H. W., 72, 81

111

Calamur, K., 2
Cambodia
    human rights violations in, 12–17
    killing fields, 14–15, 62, 65
    reengaging, 74–75
Cameroon
    jihadism in, 83
    persecution of homosexuals in,
        102–103, 104
Canyon de Chelly, water scarcity at,
    32–34
Cargo cults, 46
Case studies
    Bosnia's Omarska Concentration
        Camp, 69–74
    Cambodia's Killing Fields, 62, 65
    The Chibok Girls and Boko Haram,
        82–85
    Child Abuse/Neglect and Sex Traffick-
        ing in the United States, 79–82
    Ethiopia's Red Terror, 41–45
    Europe's Missing Refugee Children,
        85–89
    Food Insecurity in Somalia, 27–32
    Genocide in Darfur, 65–69
    India's "Unknown Insurgency," 48–51
    Kibera and Global WASHES, 23–27
    Refugees in New Guinea, 45–48
    Water Scarcity at Canyon de Chelly,
        32–34
Casey, George (General), 40, 55
Chad, 65, 66, 83, 85
Chain of Hope Rehabilitation Center, 105
Champions. See Passionaries
Chatterjee, R., 78
Chibok girls, abduction by Boko Haram,
    82–85
Children's rights, 77–91
Chinese rights abuse, 100–101
Choi-Fitzpatrick, A., 81
Christy, B., 67–68, 78
Cilliers, J., 83
Citak people (Indonesia), 39
Clans, patrilineal, in Somalia, 28–30
Coates, T., 32
Collins, S., 18
Colonial constructions in New Guinea, 46
Colorado Coalition for Genocide Aware-
    ness and Action (CCGAA), 73
Coloroso, B., 62
Committee of 2008, 98
Community-based organizations (CBOs),
    25–27
Concentration camps
    Jasenovac (Slavonia), 69, 70
    Mauthausen (Austria), 59–61
    Omarska (Bosnia), 69–74

Sremska Mitrovica (Serbia), 69, 70
    Stara Gradiška (Croatia), 70
Core–periphery relations, 67, 83
Covenants/conventions, 9
Crimes against humanity
    Holocaust, 59–61, 69–74, 79
    value-mediated/emotionally sensitive
        rights-related interventions,
        74–75
    See also Ethnic cleansing/ethnocide;
        Genocide
Crowe, R., 52
Cultural cleansing, 51, 97
Culture of terror, 43
Cure Violence Initiative, 54–55
Cyberwarfare, 40

Daasanach people (Kenya), 21
Dachau Mauthausen War Crimes Trial,
    59–61
Dank, M., 80
Danner, M., 71
Darfur
    genocide in, 65–69
    Justice and Equality Movement in,
        67
    reengaging, 75
Darfur Liberation Front, 67
Debate and discourse, 7
Declarations if rights, 9, 82
de Marie Heungoup, H., 84, 103
Democratic Republic of Congo, 68, 78,
    99–100
Desert Dies, A (Asher), 34
Deshpande, V., 78
d'Estrée, C., 84
de Waal, A., 66
Dignity, 9, 11
Dikwa refugee camp, 86
Djibouti, 28
Doino, W., Jr., 98
Donald, B. 88
Downs, J., 32–33
Dubowitz, H., 90
Duman, R., 5, 73
Duncan, P., 87

Ecotact organization, 25
Education, enabling right of, 9
Eigruber, A., 61
El Porvenir, 22
El Salvador, human rights violations in,
    39–40
Ensign, M. 85
Environmental justice and women's
    rights, 18–19
Equality/equity, essential principles of, 9

Eritrea
    marginalization of, 42
    Peasant March on, 43
Ethiopia's Red Terror, 41–45
Ethnic cleansing/ethnocide
    in Bosnia, 69–74
    Cambodia's killing fields, 62–65
    Holocaust, 3, 59–62, 69–74
Ethnic groups, marginalization of, 42, 46,
    66–67
Ethnicity, fluid nature of, 66
European child refugees, disappearance
    of, 85–89
European Union (countries), 85, 86, 88
Expeditionary diplomacy, 101

Famine, political/politicizing process of, 67
Farmar, S., 3
Farmer, P., 10
Faul, M., 82
Ferhatić, I., 73
Feticide in India, 77–78
Finley, B., 54
"Flying toilets" of Kibera, 25
Food insecurity in Somalia, 27–32
Forced labor
    in Ethiopia (Dergue government), 43,
        44, 52, 54
    in Pol Pot regime, 13–14
Forced migrants, rights violations of,
    12–17
Forced to Flee: Human Rights and
    Human Wrongs in Refugee Home-
    lands (Van Arsdale), 41, 69
Fracture zones, 52, 100
Fraser, S., 87
Freedom of expression, artistic, 19
Friedlander, E., 5
Fur people (Sudan), 66

Gabiam, N., 87
Gallagher, A., 82
Galtung, J., 10
Gambia, The
    persecution of homosexuals in, 103
    sanctions against, 104–105
Garber, S., 75
Gay rights, 19, 101–106
Gender and negotiated identity, intersec-
    tion of, 19
Gender-based violence in Nigeria, 83
General Carter Ham, 40
Genocide
    Bosnia's Omarska concentration
        camp, 69–74
    Cambodia's killing fields, 14–15, 62,
        65

    in Darfur, 65–69
    infanticide as, 78
    Nazi war crimes against the Jews,
        59–62
Ghosh, S., 10
Girl in the River (Obaid-Chinoy), 89
Glaser, S., 36
Glenny, M., 69–70
Global fractures, 52, 55
Global Greengrants, 19
Global human rights
    defining, 3–5
    passionaries, case studies, and activ-
        ism, 5–6
    people, processes, and principles, 5
Global WASHES Program, 26–27
Goldberg, S., 106
Gordon, Charles (General), 66
Gray, F., 1–2, 5
Greene, P., 105
Guantanamo Prison, 51
Guatemala Scholars Network, 99
Guatemalan Forensic Anthropology
    Foundation, 99
Gun violence in the United States, initia-
    tive against, 54–55
Gündogdu, A., 12
Gutman, R., 71
Guzel, M., 87

Haile-Mariam, Mengistu, 41–45, 53
Hailu, T., 41
Haing Ngor: A Cambodian Odyssey
    (Ngor), 12, 62
Ham, Carter (General), 40, 97
Hammer, J., 52, 82, 85
Hammond, L. C., 42, 45
Hammons, C., 41
Hance, J., 31
Heller, K., 19
Heller, M., 51–52
Higher 15 Prison (Addis Ababa), 53–54
Hilal, M., 68
Hill, C. R., 74–75
Hitchcock, M., 21
Holocaust, 3, 59–62, 69–74, 79
Holy Spirit Mobile Forces, 3
Honig, J., 70
Honor killing, 89–90
Hukanović, R., 72, 73
Human Rights and Special Prosecutions
    (HRSP) Section, US Department of
    Justice, 49
Human Rights Campaign, 104–105
Human rights champions. See Passionar-
    ies
Human Trafficking Center (Denver), 84

Huoy, C. M., 13, 15, 16
Hygiene, entrepreneurial approach to (Kenya), 25–26

India
    child abuse achievements in, 91
    feticide in, 77–78
    Naxalite insurgency in Chhattisgarh State, 48–51
Indonesia, 45–46
Inequality, structural, 9–11, 46
Infanticide as genocide, 78
Institutional innovations as obligated actions, 99–100
International Convention on the Elimination of All Forms of Racial Discrimination, 9
International Covenant on Civil and Political Rights, 104
International Criminal Court, 67
International Gay and Human Rights Commission, 104
International Society for the Prevention of Child Abuse and Neglect (ISPCAN), 88, 90–91
Invisible Children campaign, 3
Islam, 28, 30, 66, 82, 87, 103
Islamic Court Union (ICU), 30–31
Islamic State (ISIS), 41, 51, 78, 82, 87, 97
Istanbul Declaration of 2010/Istanbul II, 2012, 32

Jahanbegloo, R., 97
Jammeh, Y., 103
Janjaweed, 65, 68, 75
Jasenovac concentration camp, 70
Jihadist violence, 28, 87, 97. *See also* Islamic State (ISIS)
Joffé, R., 18
Johns Hopkins School of Medicine, 1
Junge, D., 18
Justice, 9–11
Justice and Equality Movement (Darfur), 67

Kameny, F., 106
Kampuchea. *See* Cambodia
Kane, John (Judge), 53
Kappeler, H., 98
Karadžić, R., 72
Karma, M., 50
Kasparov, G., 98
Kato, D., 103
Kefetegna 15 prison (Addis Ababa), 53
Kempe Center for the Prevention and Treatment of Child Abuse and Neglect, 81

Kenya, water and sanitation rights issues in, 23–27
Kerry, J., 27, 78, 82, 104
Ketema, K., 53
Khao-I-Dang refugee camp, 17
Khmer Rouge, 12–17, 62–64
Kibera (Kenya), 23–27
Kibera Working Group, 24–25
Killing Fields, The, 17, 62
Kim, J., 12
Kirksey, E., 46–47
Klingbiel, M., 24
Knauft, B., 46
Kony, J., 3, 5, 68
Kristof, N., 69, 90
Kumar family, 77

Lembembe, E. O., 103
Lesbian rights activism in Africa, 103–105
Lewis, T., 14
Libya, 66
Light/The Holocaust and Humanity Project, 74
Lively, S., 102
Loeb, K., 22, 24, 26
Lomalinga, M. M., 21
Lord's Resistance Army (LRA), 2–3, 68, 78
Loyd, A., 48, 50

Mahdist revitalization movements, 66
Mai Misham (Ethiopia), 44
Majina Ufanisi organization, 25
Management Sciences for Health, 97
Maoist militants in India's Chhattisgarh State, 48–51
Marginalization of indigenous residents/ ethnic groups, 42, 46, 66–67
Martin, B., 106
Mason, G., 74
Mauthausen, Austria, concentration camp, 59–61
Max, S., 2, 99
May, S., 2
Mayen, D., 61
McArthur, Douglas (General), 40
McGhee, T., 54
McGinness, H. 98
Megellas, J., 3
Melton, G. B., 80
Messianic movements, 46–47
Metzler, B., 5
Milosević, S., 72
Mitchell, G., 80
Modern art and freedom of expression, 19
Modern slavery, 81
Modi, N., 78

Mosley, D., 101–102
Mumbai, 26
Mutter, P., 87
Muyu people (Indonesia), 46, 48

Naím, M., 52
Narang, S., 77
Navajo of Canyon de Chelly, 32–34
Nazis, 59–61, 69, 98
Naxalites, 48–51, 52
Ndjio, B., 102
Necessities of life (provision rights),
    21–23
Negotiated identity and gender, 19
New Guinea, refugees in, 45–48
Ng, D., 19
Ngor, H., 12–18, 62–64
Nicaragua, provision rights through El
    Porvenir, 22
Niebling, A. L., 97
Niger, 83, 85
Nigeria
    gender-based violence in, 83, 85
    human rights imperative in, 84
    struggle of the LGBTQ community in,
        105
Night commuters, 2–3, 78
Night doctors, 1–2
Night (Wiesel), 3
Nockerts, R. A., 96
Nogwaza, N., 103
Nol, L., 63
Nong Chan refugee camp, 71
Nonmalevolence, 9
Nordstrom, C., 43, 52, 100
Nossiter, A., 83
Nuba Mountains (Sudan), 61, 98
Nyawara, J., 22

O'Flaherty, H., 98
O'Neill, T., 47
Obaid-Chinoy, S., 18, 90
Obama, B., 81, 84
Obligated actions/obligation, 9
    compassion and risk taking in, 98–99
    defining, 95–96
    institutional innovations and political
        diplomacy, 99
    interventions against anti-gay legisla-
        tion and persecution, 104–106
    persistence of, 74
    worldwide structural violence and,
        96–97
Okparanta, C., 105
Old war–new war dichotomy, 40–41
Orang hutan (Javanese pejorative term
    for Papuan peoples), 45

Orizio, R., 41–42
Ottoman Empire, 52

Palestinian refugees, 87
Palmyra, destruction of, 18, 51
Pankhurst, R., 45
Papua, Indonesia, 45–46
Papua New Guinea, refugees, 45–48
Papuan Freedom Organization (*Organ-
    isasi Papua Merdeka*), 47–48
Passionaries (human rights champions),
    5, 97–101
    Amy Lynn Niebling, 97
    Emmanuel Weyi, 99–100
    Frank Kameny, 106
    Garry Kasparov, 98
    General Carter Ham, 40
    George Tuto, 98
    Haing Ngor, 12–18
    Helen Abyei, 61
    Irena Sendler, 79
    Jockin Arputham, 26
    Monsignor Hugh O'Flaherty, 98
    Nicholas Winton, 89
    Roz Duman, 73
    Saba Qaiser, 89–90
Patrilineal clans in Somalia, 28–30
Paul, J., 81
Peasant March on Eritrea, 43
Pol Pot, 13, 18, 45, 64–65
Polaris Project, 79
Political diplomacy, 99–100
Pope Francis, 19, 106
Pornographic violence, 41
Power, 68
Power, S., 67
Power of Hope, 26
Practical Action, 24
Pragmatic humanitarianism, 95–96
Pran, Dith, 17, 62
Property rights, 10
Protocols, 9
Provision rights, 7, 21–38
    food insecurity in Somalia, 27–32
    Kibera and global WASHES, 23–27
    as necessities of life, 21–23
    securing Somalia's fisheries, 36–37
    water scarcity at Canyon de Chelly,
        32–34
    World Food Programme in South
        Sudan, 35–36
Prunier, G., 66, 67, 68
Puttnam, D., 17

Radical Jihadi Islam, 28, 87, 97
Raymond, N., 25
Red Terror, Ethiopian, 41–45

Refugees
    Cambodian, 12–17
    Eritrean, 35
    European child refugees, disappearance of, 85–89
    in Papua New Guinea, 45–48
    Somali, 28, 30
    South Sudanese, 35
Rights endeavor, fields of, 18–19
Rights resources, human, network, and funding, 8
Rights violations, and structural violence, 11–12
Rights-based research, important outcomes of, 9
Rogers, C., 34, 51
Rotary International, 21, 24, 25
Rwanda, 100

Safe Environment for Every Kid (SEEK), 90
Salafism, 82, 103
Salama, V., 97
Saldaña, J., 22
Samouillet de Gomez, E., 33
Sampson, R., 32
Samuels, A., 81
Sanitation, provision right to, 22, 23–27
Santora, M., 35
Saving Face, 18
Schanberg, S., 17
Scharer, P., 102, 103
Schoorl, J. W., 46
Secure Fisheries (Somalia), 36
SEEK model, 90
Segmentary lineage system, 29
Selassie, H., 41
Sen, A., 10, 11–12
Sen, H., 74–75
Sendler, I., 79
Sex trafficking in the United States, 79–82, 91
Sexual abuse of children, 80
Sharia law, 30
Sharma, A., 49–50
Shay, S., 28–30
Shea, N., 21
Shekau, A., 83
Sihanouk, N., 63
Singh, M., 49
Skloot, R., 1
Slum Dwellers International, 26
Slumdog Millionaire, 26
Slutkin, G., 54–55
Smith, D. R., 41, 101
Smith, M., 31
Social franchising, 26

Societal violence and warfare
    disease-control approach to urban violence, 54–55
    effective legal action against, 53–54
    Ethiopia's Red Terror, 41–45
    global fractures and, 52
    Naxalite insurgency in Chhattisgarh State (India), 48–51
    New Guinea refugees, 45–48
    torture as, 51
Somali Supreme Islamic Courts Council (SSICC), 30
Somalia
    food insecurity in, 27–32
    patrilineal clans in, 28–30
    securing fisheries in, 36–37
    segmentary lineage system in, 29
Sorame, A., 48
Sosa, Jorge, 49
South Africa, 42
South Africa's Forum for the Empowerment of Women, 105
South Sudan, World Food Programme in, 35–36
Spectacular violence, 43, 54, 96
Sphere of autonomy, 10
Srebrenica genocide, 70
Sreenivasan, H., 19
Srinivasa, C., 49–51
Stara Gradiška concentration camp, 70
Stith, J., 80–81
Stone, L., 23, 27
Stonewall Inn, 106
Structural inequality, 9–11, 46
Structural violence, 2, 72
    in concentration camps, 59–61, 69–74
    effective legal prosecution of, 53–54
    in Ethiopia, 43–44
    Khmer Rouge and Cambodian genocide, 13–17
    theory of, 10–12, 51–52
    worldwide situation regarding, 96–97
Subianto, P., 47
Sudan
    personal violence in, 39
    water resource assessment project in, 34
Sudan People's Liberation Movement (SPLM), 35, 61
Sudanese Liberation Army (SLA), 67
Sufi Islam, 103
Suicide bombers, kidnapped girls as, 85
Syria, war and refugee issues, 86–88

Tanzania, 100
Taparia, P., 91
Taylor, J., 59

Tenth Circle of Hell, The (Hukanović), 72
Terror, culture of, 30, 43
Thompson, M., 97
Tigray (Ethiopia), 42
Timor-Leste, 100
Torture, as form of societal violence, 51
Townsend, M., 85, 88
Transgender rights, 19
Tree of Rights, 7–10, 11, 21, 40, 49, 55, 74, 85, 101, 106
Trelleborg (Sweden), 88
Trierweiler, V., 105
Truman, H., 40
Turning Points LLC, 33–34
Tuto, G., 98–99
Tutu, D., 105–106
Twiss, S. B., 4

Uganda
    AIDS epidemic in, 55
    human rights initiatives in, 105
    human rights violations in, 2–3
    LRA in, 68, 78
    persecution of homosexuals in, 101–102, 103, 104
    treaty with, 100
Umar, H., 85
UN Convention on the Rights of the Child, 82
Under the Udala Trees (Okparanta), 105
UNICEF, 23, 27
United States, child abuse, neglect, and sex trafficking in, 79–82
Unterberger, A., 5, 12
Urban violence, disease-control approach to, 54–55
US Army Field Manual on Intelligence Interrogations, 51
USAID (United States Agency for International Development), 105
Ustaše, 69–70

Value-mediated rights, 10
Van Arsdale, P. W., 10, 14, 37, 41, 43, 46–47, 96, 101
Varisco, D., 18
Vietnam War, 63
Violence
    personal violence linked with social violence, 39–55
    pornographic, 41

societal. *See* Societal violence and warfare
structural, 2, 10–12, 51–52. *See also* Structural violence
urban, disease-control approach to, 54–55
worldwide situation, 96–97
Vogt, W., 11
Vulliamy, E., 71, 73

Waller, T., 70
War crimes, expanded international discussions on, 51
Warfare
    asymmetrical, 30, 40–41, 47, 55, 87
    old war–new war dichotomy, 40–41
    and social violence, 39–55
Warsaw Ghetto, 79
WASH (water, sanitation, hygiene), improvement movement, 22–23, 25–27
Water Diviner, The (Crowe), 52
Water, provision right to, 21–22, 27
Water scarcity at Canyon de Chelly, 32–34
Waterston, A., 96
Weak cultural relativism, 4, 10, 12
Weir, P. 81
Weiwei, A., 19
Welaratna, U., 63–64
Wells, H. G., 1
Werner, S., 91
West, C., 106
West Garfield, Chicago, 55
Weyi, E., 99–100
Wiesel, E., 3
Wieseltier, L., 18
Wings Foundation, 80
Winton, N., 89
Wolf, K., 3
Women's rights, 18–19, 105. *See also* Honor killing; Lesbian rights activism
World Heritage Sites, destruction of, 18
World War II, 3, 79

Yacoub, S. N., 97
Yemen (Sanaa), 18
Yogi, Thadius (General), 47
Yousafzai, M., 91

Zavis, A., 100
Zegota, 79